MODERN
ENGLISH ESSAYS

EDITED BY ERNEST RHYS

Frederic Harrison.

MODERN
ENGLISH ESSAYS
VOLUME ONE

ATHENÆUM
WALTER PATER
MATTHEW ARNOLD
CHARLES KINGSLEY
ALGERNON SWINBURNE
RICHARD HOLT HUTTON
RALPH WALDO EMERSON
JAMES RUSSELL LOWELL
FREDERIC HARRISON
WALTER BAGEHOT
EDWARD DOWDEN
MARK PATTISON
SPECTATOR

1922
LONDON & TORONTO
J. M. DENT & SONS LTD.
NEW YORK: E. P. DUTTON & CO.

INTRODUCTION

THE English essay has gone through some critical changes in the last fifty years and more, and these volumes are an attempt to put into a plain sequence the course it has run. Matthew Arnold published in 1867 his *Essays in Criticism*, and John Morley took over in the same year the editorship of *The Fortnightly Review*; and they recall that in the sixties of last century the modern essay attained its majority. In *The Fortnightly*, the old *Cornhill*, *The Saturday Review*, and *The Spectator* appeared much of the best work of the later Victorian essayists. They sustained the tradition of the great essay of an earlier period, as written by Gifford, Jeffrey, De Quincey, Carlyle, and the *Edinburgh* and *Quarterly* reviewers, who were capable of writing a review as long as a novel. But they remembered too the lighter mode of the familiar essay written by Addison and Steele, or by Hazlitt and Elia. *The Fortnightly* itself, not having the quarterly accommodation (it was issued first in fortnightly and then in monthly numbers), tended to lessen the space allotted, in spite of its editor's own virile and sustained mode. His *Burke*, which appeared in his own first volume for 1867, was on the old quarterly scale printed in three instalments, and some

of his essays on French writers were still longer.
But the men he gathered round him—Frederic
Harrison, Walter Bagehot, Cotter Morison, W. K.
Clifford, Swinburne and Philip Gilbert Hamerton
among them—cut their articles to monthly measure;
and we do not suppose that the editor incited them
to run to his own lengths.

This new stringency of the periodical page was
yet more likely to be felt in a magazine like *The
Cornhill*, which set out to be entertaining first and
intellectual afterwards. In its earlier volumes there
are solid contributions from Leslie Stephen, who
was its editor for some years, Matthew Arnold,
and other major essayists; but in style and attack,
and economy of expression, they mark a change.
And when we come to the weekly reviews, and discover men of the old " quarterly " calibre, men like
Leslie Stephen's elder brother, Fitzjames Stephen
(who became a famous judge), adapting themselves
to a middle article, and making it more damaging
than a quarterly review, we realise that the critical
headquarters have shifted from the quarterly to the
monthly and weekly reviews.

Whether as editor or miscellanist, John Morley
is one of the master-spirits of the transition
from the earlier to the later Victorians. He writes
strong idiomatic English, alive as he is to the play
of French ideas. We realise how far he has moved
when we read his account of Condorcet, and follow
it by his estimate of Carlyle. In idea, he is nearer
to Diderot than to Carlyle; and in a sense, as

his plea for the eighteenth-century spirit in the
Condorcet pages shows, he is nearer to that period
than to the early Victorian time. It is interesting
to date him, as we may by one tell-tale passage of
that essay. " The Rousseau of these times is Thomas
Carlyle," he says, " and their method is the same.
With them, thought is an aspiration, justice a sentiment, society a retrogression." He is impressed by
the cruelty of sentimentalism, and speaks of Rousseau's disciple, Robespierre. " The Reign of Terror
was the work of men whom Rousseau had fired,
and who were not afraid to wade through oceans
of blood to the promised land. We too," he declares,
and it sounds prophetic, " have seen the same result
of sentimental doctrine in the life of the battle-
field, the retrograde passion for methods of repres-
sion, the contempt for human life, the impatience of
orderly reform." One more sentence gives us the
true Morley antithesis: " We begin with intro-
spection and the eternities, and end in blood and
iron "; a sentence that G. K. C. might have been
pleased to write. Because of the scale to which
his essays were drawn Lord Morley lies rather
outside the bounds of these miniature collections:
but his influence was paramount fifty years ago
and we need to mark it in the chronological chart.

For a single example of a transition essay we
may go to Mark Pattison's on Montaigne, which
is well calculated in subject, critical power and
intellectual treatment to satisfy the modern canon.
He too, like Morley, wrote on literature with a

sense of history behind the man and the writer, and with a certain philosophy behind his surface estimate. But even better than John Morley writing on Carlyle or Macaulay, Mark Pattison writing on Montaigne, who was congenially endowed, by time and providence, to be the Father of the Essay, enables us to fix on a definite landmark. And indeed, if we hold the essay to be a form naturally conditioned by the amount a reader can read, savour and enjoyably digest at one sitting, we may safely let the French essayist guide him. That assignment indeed was Montaigne's measure. He had a sense of the natural man's needs, who wishes to be entertained, and not to be lectured, or over-dosed in the moral zeal of the essayist.

We are obliged to think of Montaigne as we try to anatomise the converser's art he practised. Of the essay as he wrote it one of his critics reminds us that if "the word is late, the thing is ancient." He would relate it to Socrates and Sirannez the Persian. The *discours* of his French contemporaries, the *discorsi* of the Italian writers, were of the same genre; but Montaigne made it more of a causerie, less of a treatise. Himself was the premise. "I consider myself variously." "I present myself standing and lying." "It is a perfect thing for a man to know how to enjoy loyally his being." "Let death find me planting cabbages." Life and death; how he lived, what he thought; or how other men, like unto himself, were affected, were his topics. He wishes us to take him for a simple *causeur* and his essays for a conversation with his reader. As has been said by a French critic, his essay on conversation or the art of conferring (viii. Book 3) is the quintessence of his whole book; Pascal called him the incomparable author of that art—" l'art de conférer."

Of exact chronology, the essay, it must be admitted, is apt to make light; because it is a wilful eccentric creature in its movements. "What is six winters? They are quickly gone." The original essayist chooses his own time. His contemporaries are Montaigne, Bacon, Fuller, Addison, Steele, Lamb, Hazlitt, Carlyle, Arnold, Morley; not to reckon later writers and our present essayists. By mere date you may range Henley writing of Hazlitt with Mrs. Meynell or Max Beerbohm. Yet are they dynasties apart in one sense, though they rub shoulders in another.

> The showes of minds are chang'd, and breasts conceave,
> At one time motions, which anon they leave,
> And others take againe.

This is to imply that the essay, like the lyric, has no positive calendar. An Elia, an Augustine Birrell; a Beddoes, a Blake, occur; and make light of your chronology.

This is one reason why the essay, like human nature, is so entertaining and unaccountable. Ostensibly it wears the fashion of its time—hat and coat and collar. At heart, it is a vagabond and free spirit—" half a lay-clerk; half a Bohemian." One element in its make-up has saved it from ever holding too closely to type, or suffering the fate of Malvolio; and that is Humour. "The true tickling sense, exquisite absurdity, soul-rejoicing incongruity —has really nothing to do with types, prevailing fashions and such-like vulgarities. Sir Andrew Aguecheek is not a typical fool; he is a fool, seised in fee-simple of his folly." So says one of the most original, most agreeably related of our essayists, he that wrote *Obiter Dicta*.

Having decided that the schools and groups of essayists are not scientifically to be labelled, we go on to the next assumption, to wit, that the special type of literary essayist which abounds in this collection has its distinct brands to be recognised by its idioms and its critical attitude. Its good qualities come of its honesty and subtlety, its resolute and authentic account of its author; while its defects are obvious enough; due to high colour, excess of rhetoric and the *non-possumus* airs of the quarterly big-wigs. The tendency in the progressive relays of essayists in these five books is so far healthy, as it does show an increasingly natural mode, and a getting rid of rhetoric and the Jeffrey-cum-Gifford tradition.

If we sketched a rough and ready pedigree for the literary essay from Carlyle onwards, we should trace its devious line from his essays on Walter Scott and Voltaire, and from Macaulay's on Milton and Addison, to Mark Pattison's Montaigne, Arnold's Spinoza, in America Lowell's sharp-edged appreciation of Thoreau, Emerson's estimate of Swedenborg, Morley's of Diderot, Bagehot's of Dickens, Frederic Harrison's review at large of *Lothair*; Mr. Birrell's of Carlyle; Austin Dobson's of Goldsmith; Edmund Gosse's of Christopher Smart; George Saintsbury's of Scott and Dumas; Henley's of Hazlitt; Swinburne's of Landor; Leslie Stephen's of Richardson's novels; and so to such tributes by living men as that of Mr. Conrad to Marryat and Fenimore Cooper, G. K. C.'s to Dickens, and Mr. Santayana's to Shelley. Once the critic is among his live contemporaries, he is apt to lose the exact thread in the tangle of pens and personalities.

The present collection is meant, then, to be suggestive, and not in any way exhaustive. It picks out its instances now for reasons of style and vivid treatment, now for variety of subject, now for the unmistakable Montaigne touch with an individual readjustment. Originally intended as a gallery of literary essays, it expanded as time went on to a set of essays on Life, Letters, Men, Places, Books and Characters. It is first of all an anthology of English writers; but it casts its net wide enough to bring in some American essays— just so much of a leavening as may serve to keep us in mind of the keen, robust, independent way of writing that one associates with *The Atlantic Monthly*, *The Dial*, *Scribner's Magazine*, *The Yale Review*, *The Century* and others.

Had there been space for them, one would certainly have included some American essays of places; such as Wentworth Higginson's *Oldport Wharves*, W. D. Howell's *Old Boston*, and Charles Dudley Warner's studies of a Winter Interior. But a separate anthology is due to the writers of America, which may yet be added to this English collection.

The end and aim of such an enchiridion is to arouse interest in the whole literature it draws upon; not to satisfy an errant reader or a piecemeal curiosity. What said Montaigne ?

" To judge in a writer the parts most his own and best worthy, together with the force and beautie of his minde, 'tis very requisite we know first what is his owne, and what not: and in what is not his owne, what we are beholding to him for, in consideration of his choice, disposition, ornament, and language he hath thereunto furnished. What if he have borrowed the matter and empaired the forme ? as many times it commeth to passe. Wee others that have little practise with bookes, are troubled with this, that when wee meet with any rare or quaint invention in a new poet, or forcible argument in a preacher, we dare not yet commend them, untill we have taken instruction of some wise man, whether that part be their owne or another bodies. And untill then I ever stand upon mine owne guard."

Every one in the end must stand on his own guard, and become his own anthologist.

E. R.

EDITOR'S NOTE

THIRTEEN essayists are grouped in this volume, which shows in brief the Modern English Essay's late Victorian development from the days of the old *Fortnightly Review* onwards. In 1867, John Morley—now Lord Morley—took over the editorship of that powerful organ from George Henry Lewes; and of the men associated with him, Edward Dowden, Frederic Harrison, Mark Pattison, Walter Pater, and A. C. Swinburne are represented in this group. In the same year appeared Matthew Arnold's *Essays in Criticism*, which serves as another clear landmark in the retrospect; and from its salient pages comes the characteristic Spinoza essay which opens the present text. Of the other writers, Walter Bagehot, who contributes the second essay, on Cobden, was a pioneer of the new criticism; but his earlier volumes of *Literary Studies* lie outside our bounds. He too was nurtured in the tradition of the great essay, which gives way to the shorter flights of the monthly and weekly reviews. Richard Holt Hutton was another editor-essayist, whom we associate definitely with the later *Spectator*. We have taken one unsigned *Spectator* and one *Athenæum* essay; it may be conjectured that the former bears the sign of something very like Hutton's own hand. In the same decades of last century *The Cornhill*

Magazine had on its staff some notably good essay-writers, not forgetting Leslie Stephen its sometime editor, many of whose " Hours in a Library " first saw print in its pages. But he, again, took a large canvas for his intellectual portraits of men like Richardson the novelist and Nathaniel Hawthorne, and in this collection of mixed essays he has been otherwise represented. We have made one exception, on the side of the ordinary time-measure, in order to include Mark Pattison's *Montaigne*, which is valid as a tribute to that master-essayist and as an anticipation of the newer essayists who were affected by him. Swinburne's tribute to Landor is a noble recall too of the older generation by a poet alive to the revolutionary ardour of the new; while Frederic Harrison's essay on Disraeli's novel is a curious and vigorous revelation of certain Victorian tendencies, social and political. We have added as American makeweight two essays, one in which Emerson, grown old, relates his estimate of old age; and the other in which Russell Lowell offers his searching and somewhat caustic criticism of Thoreau.

For permission to use copyright essays in this volume, special acknowledgment is due and is hereby made to Messrs. Macmillan and Co. Ltd., for R. H. Hutton's essay on John Stuart Mill from *Contemporary Thought and Thinkers,* and for Mr. Frederic Harrison's essay " The Romance of the Peerage " from *The Choice of Books.* Thanks are also rendered to the author of that volume ; and further, for Swinburne's essay on Landor, to Messrs. Wm. Heinemann.

CONTENTS

MODERN ENGLISH ESSAYS

MONTAIGNE [1]

By Mark Pattison

Montaigne supplies the French with what Shakespeare does ourselves — a perpetual topic. The *Essais* have a breadth and depth which criticism is not yet weary of measuring and re-measuring. And, notwithstanding all the excellent things that have been said on those unique effusions, doubtless there remains more still that can be said. There are some books which partake of the inexhaustible multiformity of our moral nature, and the *Essais* is one of such books. "On y trouve tout ce qu'on a jamais pensé," as one of Montaigne's admirers says.

But besides the book of essays, the author's life offers a fund for the regular investment of floating public curiosity. In this department the material for speculation is constantly on the increase. "Montaignologie" is become a science by itself. Documentary research has yielded the French antiquaries

---

[1] 1. *La Vie Publique de Michel Montaigne.* By Alphonse Grün.   2. *Nouveaux Documents Inédits ou peu connus sur Montaigne.* By J. F. Payen.

year by year a residuum of "new fact." Each
small bit of ore passes in its turn through the
smelting-pot of public discussion, till the portion
of precious metal it contains is extracted from it.
When the grains have accumulated to a heap, comes
a new "étude," which digests and arranges all the
facts new and old into a consistent whole. One of
these is now before us, and gives occasion to our
present notice. We shall confine our remarks to
Montaigne's life. We are not going to re-dissect
the *Essais*.

We have likened Montaignesque to Shakespearean criticism, as two perennial streams supplied
each by its glacier on the far off mountain-top.
The writings of the two men stand in marked
contrast as sources for their biography. From
Shakespeare's plays nothing can be gathered about
Shakespeare. The great charm of Montaigne's
Essays is their egotism. They are a transcript of
his mind. "Ce ne sont mes gestes que j'escris;
c'est moy, c'est mon essence." When Henri III.
told him that he "liked his book," then, replied
Montaigne, "Your majesty must needs like me.
My book is myself." But it is the man—his habits
and opinions, his tastes and likings that we find
there, not his history. The biographers, therefore,
have endeavoured to discover elsewhere the body
belonging to this soul. They have ransacked
libraries and archives to resuscitate something of
a frame-work of bone and muscle to all this sentiment. They have had some success. Indeed they

have had as much success as could be expected, considering that it was known beforehand that all that could possibly be discovered lay within fixed limits. They have ascertained dates, distinguished the members of his family, and altogether given a local colouring and verification of the course of his private life. They have not turned the literary lounger into a careworn statesman, or a fighting captain of the forces of the League. In this as in many other cases, all the efforts of inquiry have but repeated the lineaments of the traditional and received biography. Such labour, however, is not thrown away. We are not to propose a paradox, or a revolution in opinion, as the only results worth arriving at. If we can deepen the lines, or freshen the colours, cover a scar made by time, or remove a little gathered dust, we do our part towards maintaining the Gallery of Worthies. It is only when the original portrait is discovered not to have been a likeness, that we should paint it over again.

The great feature of Montaigne's life, as impressed on his *Essais,* was, that it was a country life. Early in 1571, at the age of thirty-seven, he withdrew to his estates in Perigord—"with full purpose, as much as lay in me, not to trouble myself with any business, but to pass in repose so much of life as remaineth to me." [1] My design is, he repeats in the Third Book written after 1580, " de passer doulcement, non laborieusement, ce que me reste de vie." [2] It was solitude at first. He declined

[1] I. 8.   [2] III. 9.

society, and occupied himself with his family, his books, the care of his property. This lasted some little time, but his temper was sociable, and he found he could not support solitude. " Je suis tout au dehors, et en évidence; nay à la societé, et à l'amitié." [1] And he disliked the cares of the *ménage*. He sought distraction, therefore, in the company of his neighbours, in travelling, and in writing. He wished retirement, not solitude. What he would shun was the pressure of business, not crowds. Repeated tours—one to Italy—a journey or two to Paris about the publication of his *Essais*, and his mayoralty at Bordeaux, in 1582, forced on him against his wishes, are the principal events of his life after his retirement. Such at least was the received biography. Nor had any of the disinterred facts disturbed the repose of the picture. His diary of his tour in 1580, written in Italian, was found at Montaigne one hundred and eighty years after his death, and was published in 1774. Now De Thou had said in the 104th book of his history, that Montaigne was at Venice when he received the news of his election to the mayoralty. This journal enables us to correct De Thou. It was at the baths of Lucca, on the 7th of September, in the morning. The letter was dated Bordeaux, August 2nd, and had followed him into Tuscany, by way of Rome. Such *incrementa* reassure, instead of invalidating, history.

An attempt, however, is now made to wrest

[1] III. 9.

from us the Montaigne of our youth, the "Gentilhomme Perigourdin"; to tear him from the frame
in which he was set in our memory and our affections, from the "librairie" and "chambre d'études
au troisième étage" of the old "manoir" of Montaigne, and to make of him—good heavens!—to
make of him a man of business, a man about court.
M. Grün's volume is entitled *La Vie Publique de
Michel Montaigne.* The titles of its several chapters
are:—Ch. 2. "De la Conduite publique de M."
Ch. 3. "M. Magistrat." Ch. 4. "Relations de
M. avec la Cour." Ch. 5. "M. Chevalier de
l'Ordre de S. Michel." Ch. 6. "M. Gentilhomme
Ordinaire de la Chambre du Roi." Ch. 9. "M.
Negociateur Politique." Ch. 10. "M. Militaire."
Ch. 11. "M. aux Etats de Blois."

Such a metamorphosis of our prose Horace, the
man of whom "la liberté et l'oysiveté sont les
maîtresses qualités" [1] into a hardworking man of
office, dressed in the imperial livery trimmed with
red tape, is one of those harlequin tricks which
paradoxical biographers try upon us from time to
time. We have been lately told that Tiberius has
been slandered by Tacitus; that the world was
never better off than under Caracalla; and that
Henry VIII. was the victim of domestic infelicities.
On examining M. Grün's volume we find there
is no more evidence for the Imperialist trans-
formation of Montaigne than there is in the other
three instances. There is in M. Grün's mode of

[1] III. 9.

arranging his facts, indeed, a certain degree of art, but it is the skill of the special pleader. It is the argumentation of the Palais de Justice, not of the Court of History. The highest praise is due to French archæologists for their zeal of research, but they cannot, apparently, apply their discoveries. Such a piece of historical reconstruction as this *Vie Publique de Montaigne,* in which hypothesis and imagination are the principal architects, would not stand a chance of a hearing in Germany. We shall add, however, that this attempt to disguise Montaigne has not passed unchallenged in France. With all the authority of his own name, and of the body to which he belongs, M. Villemain has in the gentlest language pointed out that the critic's evidence will not bear all the weight of his conclusions. To no man could this task fall with so much propriety as to Villemain. His own earliest step into publicity was an *éloge* of Montaigne. It was in 1812 that he carried off, though the youngest of the competitors, the prize proposed by the Académie Française on this subject. It is proof of the national feeling for Montaigne that the first of French living critics, after having made the whole circuit of his country's literature, returns after half a century to the object of his youthful devotion.

It is not our intention to controvert M. Grün's conclusions. It is unnecessary even to examine his reasoning. It is not merely that his evidence is inadequate, but his case is bad to begin with.

His intention is worse than his argumentation. An able legist, government *employé*, and ex-chief-editor of the *Moniteur*, he brings into literature the habits and prepossessions of his position. The Academy, and the established reputations, look coldly on the administration from which they are systematically excluded. It is not from republican principle, from antipathy to despotism that they do so—it is from the repugnance which the lettered and cultivated man feels for the official man who is not so. Times are changed since the statesmen in France were the writers—when to be a journalist conferred *portefeuilles*. Statistics is your only reading now. Point and epigram, and sparkling style—how childish to be governed by such instruments. Let us have men of business, and have done with *mots*. All the great men—Sully, Richelieu—have been able administrators. And the great writers too? "To be sure," is the answer, "and in proof there is Montaigne. You think he was a rustic recluse, who forswore the court for his old Gascon château, but you are entirely mistaken." This baseless theory is not worth refuting. The real value of M. Grün's *Vie de Montaigne* is as a painstaking collection of the facts at present known. It includes all the new discoveries, except those that have come to light since its publication—and though it is only six months old, there is already a considerable harvest.

It would we conceive be more than individual error, it would be a fundamental misconception of

7

the character of French literature, to lose sight of the following general distinction. The literature of the *Siècle* is the literature of a court circle. It is fashionably dressed, it is modish, Parisian. It comes not from the study, but from the world. From a world, however, of etiquette, of polished intrigue, a world with all its licence, yet circumscribed by conventional morals. Thought and judgment are there, but they are conformed to a certain superficial standard of good society. In a word, it is the literature of the salons of Paris and Versailles. In contrast with this, the few great pieces of literature of the previous age, from Rabelais down to Pascal, were the offspring of the cloister, the château, or the wayside. They are the *Vox clamantis in deserto.* Their superior force and originality derive directly from the rude independence of character, which was generated by that free and unformal life. In Montaigne especially, it is the force of individual character, coming out on us in every page of his book, that charms. He stands in awe of no Café Procope, has heard of no rules of writing, he is not composing. He has the hardy and fearless spirit of a man who has no one to please but himself. " J'ay une âme libre et tout sienne, accoustumée à se conduire à sa mode." [1] He complains somewhere that his times had not produced any great men. Greatness, to be manifested to the world, depends on the conjunction of natural endowment with opportunity, and must needs be rare. But

[1] II. 17.

we may surely say that the average stamp of the men of that day was great. Compared with the feminine uniformity of the shaved and tailor-made man of later court-dress days, how grand are the bearded seigneurs of the sixteenth century! Intrepid, not lawless; disciplined in the school of action and suffering; and conscious of all the restraints that limit human will, these men had made their acquaintance with law in its grandest form, not in that degenerate artificial shape in which the victim of good society alone knows it.

Montaigne was born in 1533 and died in 1592. His father's name was Pierre Eyquem. M. Gence, the writer of the life in the *Biographie Universelle*, says that the family was originally from England. That a French biographer should be willing to make over one of the greatest of his countrymen to England might surprise us. It may well do so in this instance, as the self-denial is wholly uncalled for. We cannot in honesty accept the offer. " Eyquem," or rather " Eyckem," according to the old spelling, is a compound of the common termination " ham " or " heim," and the name of that tree, which in the English vocalisation is " oak." The German " eiche," or the Flemish " ecke," come much nearer to the form in " Eyquem." Accordingly, some of the biographers have thought of looking to Flanders for the original stock of the family. It is still an open question in " Montaignologie," and M. Grün produces no evidence for his positive assertion that the name is " essentially of Gascon origin." In the course of the sixteenth century the personal was superseded by the territorial appellation. This was derived from a domain which they possessed five leagues from Bergerac, in the department of the Dordogne. The château is situated on a height — " une montagne " — " jonchée sur une tertre," he says: in this tower Montaigne was born, lived, and died. The possession of this domain was an acquisition, it should appear, which the Eyquem had only recently made; their nobility, therefore, was of very modern date. Joseph Scaliger said in an off-hand way that the father of Montaigne " était vendeur de harenc." [1] M. Grün, with the bitterness habitual to French writers when they have to speak of Scaliger, repels this as a false and malevolent insinuation. The main fact implied, however, that the ancestors of Montaigne were " marchand," and, therefore, " bourgeois," is indisputable. We must not omit, as he has recorded it himself, that he was an eleven months' child. As he was a third son of a family, now noble and not rich, his father, an excellent person, took particular pains about his education. He was put out to nurse at a poor village on the estate. Here he was kept all his infancy, with the view both of accustoming his taste to rude diet, and of inducing him to form attachments amongst the poor. His sympathy with peasant life he preserved to the last. " The poor fellows," thus he writes in a season of more than usual suffering in

[1] *Scaligerana Secunda,* p. 457.

the country, "the poor fellows whom we see all about, their heads bowed over their tasks, who never heard of Aristotle, or Cato, from them nature obtains heroic efforts of patient endurance, which may shame us who have studied in the schools. That man who is digging my garden, he has this morning buried a son, or a father perhaps. They never take to their beds but to die."

The most curious experiment made in his education was that of teaching him Latin before French. A German preceptor who could speak no French was found for him. None of the rest of the household, mother, maid, or man, were allowed to speak anything but Latin to him.

It is not to be imagined how great an advantage this proved to the whole family. My father and mother by this means learned Latin enough to understand it perfectly well, as did also those of the servants who were most with me. In short we Latined it at such a rate that it overflowed to all the neighbouring villages, where there yet remain, that have established themselves by custom, several Latin appellations of artisans and their tools. Thus I was above six years of age before I understood either French or Perigordin any more than Arabic, and without art, book, grammar, or precept, whipping or the expense of a tear, had by that time learned to speak as pure Latin as my master himself.[1]

The same attention was extended to all the minutiæ of his training. To save him from the shock of sudden awakening, some musical instrument was played by his bedside in the morning.

[1] I. 25.

Our readers will recollect the same usage in the early education of Bishop Horne, as described by his biographer Jones of Nayland.

When he quitted this careful paternal roof, it was to go to the college of Guienne at Bordeaux. At this school, quite recently established, some of the best scholars then to be found in France were masters. But as he left it at the age of thirteen, he could not have profited much by the higher scholarship which Muretus and George Buchanan were capable of communicating. As the sword belonged by birth to the eldest son, Michel, as the third, had to choose between the church and the robe. He chose, or rather his father chose for him, the latter. At thirteen he must have been incapable of choice, and he always looked to his excellent parent with a mixture of respect and affection, which disposed him to acquiesce in his least wishes. What school of jurisprudence he attended is not known. M. Grün makes it Toulouse, for he naturally wishes "Montaigne Magistrat" to have been a pupil of the celebrated Cujas. It may have been so. There is not a particle of evidence to show that it was. The solitary text is Montaigne's own declaration: "While a child, I was plunged up to the ears in law, and it succeeded."

As soon as he was qualified, his father provided him with a place in the Court of Aids of Périgueux. The law was entered there, as the army is with us, now, by purchase. We cannot stay to debate with the antiquaries the knotty point whether Montaigne's father resigned in his son's favour, or purchased him the place of some other counsellor. In 1557 the Court of Aids of Périgueux was consolidated with the Parlement of Bordeaux. And thus, at the early age of twenty-four, Montaigne was seated on the bench of a Supreme Court of Justice without either of the troublesome ceremonies of purchase or examination.

Honourable it was for a younger son; but when by the death of his father and both his brothers, Michel became himself the Seigneur de Montaigne, the long robe no longer befitted him. By these events he became a "gentleman," and carried arms, as the phrase was. Ill-natured people said in after days that Montaigne was ashamed of having been counsellor cleric, and did not like to allude to that period of his life. M. Grün is able to repel peremptorily this imputation. It proceeded indeed from later days, when Parlements were fallen, and the magistracy, especially the provincial magistrature, was looked down upon by the courtier The sneers of Balzac and the Port-Royalists are in the spirit of their own time, and are quite miscalculated for the age of L'Hospital, Pasquier, and De Thou. All Montaigne's friends, relations, and connexions—his father, uncle, brother-in-law—were parliament men. He himself married Françoise de la Chassaigne, daughter of one of the Bordelais counsellors and descendant of a parliamentary family. His most cherished friend La Boétie had been his colleague in the magistracy;

and all the friendships he retained through life had been cemented during his own parliamentary career. So much, however, is true, that Montaigne did not relish his judicial functions. This distaste had two causes: dislike of law, and dislike of the religious fanaticism which animated the magistracy of Bordeaux.

He was never really a lawyer. The plunge up to his ears had succeeded in qualifying him for a charge, but had not given him the professional dye. The biographers have exaggerated this distaste into disgust. They make Montaigne into a law reformer; they ascribe to him an enlightened jurist's view of the contradictions of the customary law, and predilection for the luminous simplicity of the civil. This, again, is to read the sixteenth century by the reflected light of '89. Montaigne imbibed the views and aims of the more enlightened jurists of his own time, but he did not project the Code Napoléon. The opinions he has left on record on this subject are very general, but they are those of a wise and humane moralist, not of a jurist. They show how much of a philosopher and how little of "a magistrate" he was. He has first an abhorrence of litigation, not less for others than himself; he declares against the multiplication of enactments, the contradictory judgments, the glosses of the commentators; but all this is in the spirit of a man of taste; revolted at the bad Latin of the Digest, and wishing to be reading his Cicero. It is a declaration against the language of law alto-

gether rather than against its abuse in chicane. He
condemns torture, and the horrible mutilations
which were practised on the bodies of the unhappy
criminals. But in this he only echoed the opinion
of all the moralists of all time, and had with him all
the great and wise of his own day. Against him,
however, were the churchmen and Rome. Those
passages in his Essays in which he pleads that all
beyond simple death is pure cruelty, presented one
of the chief obstacles to their passing the censure;
the other, we may mention, was his assigning a
high rank among Latin poets to Theodore Beza.
He eloquently denounces the practice of selling
the places in the courts of justice; and, to complete
the list, he ridicules entails, or, as he calls them,
"masculine substitutions." Sir W. Hamilton wishes
to trace this opinion of Montaigne to the tuition
of Buchanan.[1] Buchanan having quitted the
college at Bordeaux in 1542, his pupil was only
nine years old—an age at which we may doubt if
he understood what "masculine substitution" was.

In truth we believe Montaigne, when he says
of himself [2] that he knew there was such a science
as jurisprudence, and that that was all he did know.
His amusing pleading against the lawyers [3] is
nothing more than one of the many popular dia-
tribes on that traditional butt. If it proves anything,
it proves that he was no lawyer; as his vituperation

[1] Note in Hamilton's excellent edition of *Dugald Stewart*,
vol. i. p. 100.
[2] I. 24. [3] III. 13.

in the same Essay of the medical practitioners does, that he was no physician. He is, in fact, merely using the contradictions of judges and the uncertainties of medicine, to enforce his favourite topic of the feebleness of human judgment. It is as great a fallacy to class him with the enlightened publicists, who saw and laboured to remedy the monstrous evils of the French judicial system, as it would be to class him among the revolutionists of the practice of physic. The Montaigne adorers exaggerate their idol in every direction. He is great enough: he is a man of universal sympathies, but they want to make him a man of profound acquirement, which he was not—not even in his own profession. We suspect that his professional history was the common one where strong literary tastes are early imbibed. Buchanan *may* have had something to do with this—may have laid the groundwork of classic predilections which made steady application to law impossible. Montaigne followed it as a career; he got a place, discharged its duties; he never had a vocation for it, and gave it up as soon as he wanted it no longer.

The second cause of distaste for his Parliamentary functions, to which allusion has been already made, was the violence of religious faction which disturbed it. In no quarter of France had Protestantism made more progress than in Guienne and Gascony Everywhere the Parlements showed themselves the strenuous supporters of the Church. None was more untiring in the zeal for persecution than that of Bordeaux. Their registers for some years are one series of edicts, each more cruel than the last, against the professors of the new opinions. Montaigne was attached throughout to the Catholic and Royalist party. In this adhesion he never wavered, and it belonged to his characteristic frankness never to conceal it. But he was of too moderate a temper to be carried away by the passionate fanaticism of his party; too good-hearted not to execrate their cruelty; and too wise not to see that the violence of the Catholics only provoked the more obstinate resistance of the Huguenots. But wisdom and moderation are no titles to the respect of religious faction. We shall not wonder then that Montaigne, whose spirit of tolerance went far beyond even that of tolerant men in that age, was glad to terminate his connexion with a court of justice, which seemed to have totally forgotten the duty of judicial impartiality, and to have made itself the organ of an infuriated party.

All the zeal of the antiquaries has not been able to retrieve a history for the thirteen or more years during which Montaigne occupied his seat in the Parlement of Bordeaux. M. Grün goes through the principal transactions of the Court during that period—a useful *résumé* and a very proper part of a complete life, but too extensive for our purpose. The single sentence in De Thou's history, " Olim in senatu Burdigalensi assessor dignissimus," is nearly the whole that is known of thirteen years of Montaigne's life.

The second period extends from 1570 to 1582, *ætat.* 37–49, and is that portion of Montaigne's life to which he owes his immortality. This period is really marked by a long and absolute retirement in the château of Montaigne, by the composition of the *Essais*, and by two or three journeys to Paris, chiefly connected with their publication. It is concluded by a long tour into Germany, Switzerland, and Italy. M. Grün, who will not resign even this period from his "public life," interpolates into it two visits to court, which are wholly imaginary; a campaign against Henri of Navarre, which is in the highest degree improbable; and, by way of mingling pleasure with business, he exhibits his hero at the fêtes and galas which marked the progress of Catherine de Médicis in the south, in the year 1578.

The hypothetical history here spoils the authentic. The legend misleads instead of assisting the imagination. This retirement in the château of Périgueux, the solitary meditation in the turret chamber, is the canonical fact. A biographer would do good service who could paint for us in its true colours this Gascon interior. Communicative, garrulous even, as Montaigne has been about himself, what he has told us has only given us a reason for desiring to know the things he has not told us. He has made us so much his friends that we require to know all his secrets. He has drawn for us himself, his library; it is on the third floor of one of the turrets of the château. There are four stories in the turret. The first floor is the chapel; above the chapel is a bed-room with suite, appropriated to his own use. The library is above the lodging-rooms. From its three bay windows it commanded a view of nearly the entire premises, including the garden, the front as well as the base court. In the distance, the elevation on which the château stood afforded a very extensive view over a flat country. The shape of the room was that of the tower, round —all but one straight side where the chair and table were placed. From this seat the eye could command all the books as they stood ranged in five tiers of shelving round the walls: the room was sixteen paces in diameter. Opening into the library was a smaller cabinet; this was more elegantly furnished; it was fitted with a fire-place, to which he might retire in the winter. The only want he regretted was a long gallery, or " promenoir," to agitate his thoughts in by walking up and down. He could not resolve on adding this: not the cost, but the fuss, of building, deterred him. In this tower he passed the greater part of his time. There was his throne; there his rule was absolute. That only corner he preserved from the invasion of wife, children, or acquaintance. Elsewhere he possessed but a divided authority; for this reason he rejoiced that the access to his retreat was difficult, and of itself defended him from intruders. Here he lived, not studied; he did not so much read books, he says, as turn them over—he did not so much meditate as allow his reverie to follow its own course. The retirement was so strict at first as to produce melancholy and engender fantastic chimeras in his imagination. It was to allay these that he first betook himself to note down his thoughts on paper. Such was the parentage of the *Essais*.

The library, however, the imagination heated by solitary musing, the melancholy grown of long seclusion, should have given birth to a very different progeny. We might have had a *Pilgrim's Progress*, or a *Castle of Otranto*, or a third part of *Huon de Bordeaulx*, but for one quality which Montaigne brought with him into his retreat. This is the thorough good sense, the tone of the man of the world, which pervades, without being paraded, every page of the book. It is not a mere rectitude of judgment about men and things, but a judgment which has been exercised and tempered by actual trials and collisions—"a learned spirit of human dealing." But for this life-giving flavour, the *Essais* would not have been the book they are. They might still have shown the varied reading of the scholar or the amusing gossip of the egotist, but they would not have been the universal favourite of "courts, camps, and country mansions." It is this which, with all their whimsical paradox, and often commonplace moralising, makes them still instructive. In tracing this element, M. Grün's chapter, "Montaigne in his Relations with the Court," affords all the materials that are to be had. We cannot adopt his theory, which turns Montaigne into a courtier, and cuts out of his Life that period of privacy, almost cynical, which we think necessary to the conception of the *Essais*. But there is evidence enough to show, what the Essays themselves require, that Montaigne had seen much of court and courtiers before he wrote them.

The kings of France in the middle ages were surrounded by the high officers attached to their person. Their court was constituted by great functionaries. The nobles of the provinces who had no employments never approached the king except when they fought by his side, or were summoned by his order. The decay of the feudal manners, and the policy of Francis I., broke through this estrangement. He loved to surround himself with a brilliant court. The gentlemen flocked to it. They laid aside the rudeness of their manners, but they lost at the same time the independence of their character. The rivalry in luxury and expense ruined them. To maintain their fortunes they were obliged to seek office. Places were created on purpose, and the once haughty nobles fought like hungry hounds for these grants at the hands of an absolute monarch who dispensed them. This revolution was gradual. It was only in progress in the sixteenth century. But Montaigne found established the usage for French gentlemen to present themselves to the sovereign without being officially placed about his person. On succeeding to the family estates, Montaigne did like the rest. He was even appointed " Gentleman in Ordinary of the Bed-chamber," an office which did not demand residence at court, but was much sought after, and for which nobility was an indispensable qualification. His complexion, he tells us,[1] was not averse to the movement of a court. He went gladly into company; he liked city life, especially Paris. Paris had possessed his affections from his earliest youth ;[2] but these social impulses were combined with another impulse urging him to seclusion:

The solitude I love and preach is no more than what serves to retire my affections and to redeem my thoughts. I would circumscribe not my steps, but my desires. I would shun not so much the throng of men as the importunity of affairs. Local solitariness, to say truth, doth rather extend and enlarge me outwardly. I give my mind more readily to state matters, and to the world, when I am alone. At the Louvre, and in the crowd, I am apt to shrink into my own skin (*je me contrains en ma peau*). Assemblies thrust me back within myself. I never commune with my own spirit so fondly, freely, and so much apart, as in the resorts of grand company and lordly ceremonial. I go gaily into great assemblies, yet doth this coyness of judgment of which I spoke attach me perforce to privacy. Yea, even in mine own house I see people more than a good many, yet few such as I love to converse or communicate withal. Herein I exercise an unusual privilege of liberty. I cry a truce to the established courtesies so distressing to all parties, of being with my guests, and conducting them about; but each one employs himself as he pleases, and entertaineth what his thoughts affect. If I please, I remain silent, musing and reserved, without offence to my guests or friends.[3]

This picture of self-portraiture is at once true to history and to nature. We read in it the parentage of the *Essais*, to which the agitation of courts and

[1] III. 3.　　　[2] III. 9.　　　[3] III. 3.

the stillness of the recluse's cell each gave their portion. And we find in it—and in none of his self-disclosures more so—we find in it one of the secrets of genius. Nay, not only of great, but of all sound minds this is true, that for their sustentation and due nurture they require the two elements, society and solitude. No healthy life is ever lived, in which either of these is wanting. And if we turn to books—to judge of mind by its most enduring products—we see the same experience repeated from age to age. There are books enough left us by those who, having never tried to live, have shut themselves within the circle of their own meditations. Wonderful in its variety and richness is the literature of mysticism and sentiment! What a wealth of thought and feeling drawn from the pure depths of human consciousness! Again, turn to the memoir-writers and court gossips. What keen observation of manners, what infinite webs of intrigue they unravel before us, what countless characters they have distinguished! But what are the books that instruct us, that speak to us as men, that raise us, but raise us not too high for our duties and our destiny? Between the frivolous and the divine lies the truly human. Wisdom that is from above, yet that can give us light in this world! Theory without facts is not science, and moralising without experience is not wisdom. A pallid and dreary jargon is the metaphysic of the schools by the side of the tangible and experimented maxim which flowers out naturally from the intellect that has lived. But unless to this experience be added the maturing influences of meditation and self-knowledge, the result is equally one-sided. We get then that unspiritual and debasing physiology of human conduct, that so-called philosophy of courts, which leaves out of the computation of motive all that separates man from any other species of mammal. In no writer perhaps are these two elements that make up wisdom mingled in happier proportion than in Montaigne.

Little has been added by the diligence of the collectors to the glimpses of his retreat which the *Essais* themselves supply. We need not wonder that the château of Montaigne has been repeatedly visited by enthusiastic pilgrims; some of these, among whom may be included poor John Sterling, have described what they saw. But they seem to have carried with them more enthusiasm than powers of accurate observation; at least they were not able to copy correctly the sentences which Montaigne had inscribed on the cornices of his library. Some of them are characteristic: and Dr. Payen has done good service by reproducing them, as they are fast being obliterated. " Quid superbis, Terra et Cinis? Væ qui sapientes estis in oculis vestris! Ne plus sapias quam necesse est, ne obstupescas." The first six are Scripture texts. After them come the classical, of which we may give— " . . . nostra vagatur In tenebris, nec cæca potest mens cernere verum," from Lucretius; παντὶ λόγῳ λόγος ἴσος ἀντίκειται, from Sextus Empiricus. Still

MONTAIGNE

more interest attaches to an inscription in the
" cabinet du travail "; this is in Latin, and also
in a state of decay. It is to the following effect,
when the gaps have been conjecturally supplied:

In the year of Christ 1571, the 38th of his age, on
his birthday, to wit the last day of February, Michel
de Montaigne, long wearied of court slavery and
public employments, has withdrawn himself into
the bosom of the Sisters of Learning, where, in peace
and freed from care, he will pass through what little
may yet remain of a life of which the most part hath
already passed away, if only fate permit. This narrow
abode and loved ancestral retreat he hath consecrated
to his liberty, repose, and tranquillity.

If these lines be genuine they are autobiographical,
and decisive against M Grün's theory; he naturally,
therefore, wishes to think them the product of some
later hand. But he does not offer one critical argument for the suspicion he throws on them. " The
sentiment they express is too puerile for Montaigne,
and not in keeping with his habits." To bring up
a loose analogy of this sort against epigraphic evidence is simply childish in the eyes of those who
know what historical criticism is; but in this
instance it happens that the analogy itself is not
good. The inscription does but repeat that passage
in the *Essais* which we have already quoted: " Je
me retirai chez moi, délibéré autant que je pourrais
ne me mesler d'autre chose que de passer en repos
et à part le peu qui me reste de vie." Even if then
the inscription were put up by a successor, the
sentiment in it is derived from Montaigne himself,
who more than once in the *Essais* enters into this

engagement with himself to consecrate the re-
mainder of his days to studious repose. The in-
sertion of his age, and the solemn mention of his
birthday, which M. Grün thinks " puerile," appear
to us exactly in Montaigne's character. Dr. Payen
has justly remarked that he is fond of noting his
age at different epochs of his composition; that
his *Natural Theology* is dated the day of his father's
death, to whom it is dedicated; and reminds us
that Montaigne liked to use his father's cloak, not
because it fitted him, but because " il lui semblait
s'envelopper de lui." We must, however, express
our surprise that the date of this inscription should
still be left matter of argument. Surely the shape
of the letters, the style and colouring, or other
indications would serve to ascertain if the epigraph
were or were not contemporary with Montaigne.

The mention of the five tiers of shelving has
naturally suggested to our painstaking friends an
inquiry after the books which once filled them.
For though the shelves are there, and the mottoes
on the rafters above them are dimly visible, the
books are gone. Dr. Payen has here had wonderful
success. He has traced or recovered upwards of
thirty volumes which were in the possession of
Montaigne, and contain his autograph, or other
notes. The history of his twenty years' siege and
final capture of Montaigne's *Cæsar* forms of itself
a little epic, which we read in the *Débats* not long
since,[1] and one is too glad to talk of Montaigne's

[1] *Journal des Débats,* mars 1856.

Cæsar, since the other Cæsar is interdicted ground.
It tells how M. Parison, the distinguished biblio-
phile, who, with an income of £250 a year, left
behind him the astonishing collection of books
which has just been dispersed by public auction,
picked up the *Cæsar* in one of the quais bookstalls;
how he guarded it five years—not *thirty-five*, as
the *Débats* exaggerates—without breathing the
existence of the treasure—how, in 1837, Dr.
Payen, the chief of the " Montaignologues," got
scent of its existence—how he laid siege to M.
Parison's citadel on the fourth floor of a house on
the Quai des Augustins, by a series of dedications,
notes, allusions sometimes flattering, sometimes
caustic, till the final triumph in 1838, when the
stubborn possessor surrendered at discretion, yielded
up the *Cæsar*, took to his bed, and died. Had we
space we would not so curtail this bibliographical
episode. The *Cæsar*, after all, is not devoid of
interest even for our purpose. It is the Antwerp
edition (*ex Officinâ Plantinianâ*) of 1570. Montaigne had noted on it, as he did in all the books
he read, the time occupied in reading it. He commenced reading the three books *De Bello Civili*
on February 25th, and finished the *De Bello Gallico*
July 21st, in the year 1578. After the Anno
Domini he has added 44–45—figures which indicate his age at the time of reading, his birthday
being, as will be remembered, February 28th. The
marginal notes, of which there are upwards of six
hundred, do not offer much of quotable interest.

But in the minute care with which it was read, and the fact that it was read continuously between February and July, we gain some light upon Montaigne's method of using books. All his reading was not of the desultory kind we might infer from what he says of it in the Essays: " Je feuillette à cette heure un livre, à cette heure un aultre, sans ordre, et sans dessein, à pièces descousues." [1] He could, we see, at the time he was writing his *Essais*, begin a book, and return to it day after day till it was read through. In the last page he has written, in his small and fine hand, a short appreciation of the book and its author. This was his usual custom when he had finished a work. He adopted it, he says,[2] to meet the extreme treachery of his memory. This was so great that it had happened to him more than once to take up a volume which he had carefully read a few years before as if it was a new book. On comparison of the appreciation of Cæsar, which occupies thirty-six lines of close writing, with the thirty-fourth chapter of the second book of the *Essais*, we find that the essay is a greatly improved development of the annotation. Indeed, it is more than improved. The judgment passed on Cæsar in the annotation is imperfect, and fails in doing justice to him. In the essay Montaigne rises to a far higher elevation, and indicates a much more matured point of view. Now, the *aperçu*, as we have seen, was written in 1578. The *Essais* were published in

[1] III. 3.   [2] II. 10.

28

1580. Thus we gather that it was not Montaigne's habit to dismiss a book from his thoughts when he had finished it and recorded sentence on it. It might continue to occupy his meditations and grow upon his thoughts. The casual and discontinuous turning over of books, he tells of, was the external aid to a methodical and solid process of digestion.

The duties, whatever they were, of " Gentleman in Ordinary to the Bedchamber " were the only ones which Montaigne ever discharged at court. Difficulties still uncleared surround this function. Its date is uncertain, and we know not how to reconcile it with Montaigne's own assertion that he had never received from any prince a " double " either as wages or free-gift. Leaving these interesting *nœuds* to the discussion of the biographer that is to come, we have to speak of the great question of the secretaryship. For many years all the lives and *éloges* of Montaigne had repeated that he at one time filled the office of secretary to the Queen Dowager Catherine de Médicis. This would have changed the complexion of his life indeed, and would have of itself turned the scale decisively in favour of M. Grün's views. This mistake, for such it is, and nothing more, arose from the negligent, assumptive habits of the literary biographers. There is preserved a letter of instruction from the queen addressed, so it is indorsed in the MS. copy in the Bibliothèque Impériale (collection *Dupuy*), " Au roy Charles IX. peu après sa majorité." It is a piece of no little curiosity in itself. It belongs, indeed, to general history, and is as widely known as the farewell letter which another Medici addressed to his young twelve-year-old cardinal (afterwards Leo X.). But it concerns us at present, not by its contents, but by a postscript of three lines as follows: " Monsieur my son, do not take it amiss that I have made Montaigne write out this letter; I did it that you might read it better.—Catherine."

This letter made its first appearance in print in Le Laboureur's additions to the *Memoirs of Castelnau*, in 1659. Which of Montaigne's biographers may claim the credit of having transported the " new fact " into Montaigne's biography we have not ascertained. But before the beginning of the present century Montaigne's Secretariate to the Queen had become an accredited event. One of them, M. Jay, comments thus: " Those who have studied the character and manners of Catherine de Médicis, and who have read with attention the reflections of Montaigne himself on the rights and duties of princes, will easily recognise that the *Avis* are the composition of Montaigne himself." Thus history made itself as it went on through the hands of slipshod *littérateurs*. From copyist, Montaigne became author of Catherine's letter. But as soon as a discerning eye was directed to the evidence on which the " Secretariate " rested, it was seen at a glance that the identification of the amanuensis of the *Avis* with the essayist was a pure conjecture. And the indefatigable labours of Dr.

Payen have brought to light the existence of a
François Montaigne, Secretary in Ordinary of the
Chamber of the King and the Queen-Mother.
M. Grün devotes fifteen pages to the correction
of this error. It is a piece of historical reasoning
which is a fair specimen of his book. The case is
plausibly and forcibly put: but that is all. He
creates at least as much error as he rectifies. He
makes out Catherine's Montaigne to be Jacques
de Montagne, "avocat-général" at Montpellier
in 1560. The forensic skill with which the evidence is marshalled covers a quantity of conjectural
assumption which, much more than the concluding blunders, must entirely destroy M. Grün's
credit as a historical critic.

The third and last period of Montaigne's life
extends from *ætat.* 50–59. This includes a portion
of his career which may with more justice be
entitled his " public life."

He received the announcement of his nomination
to the mayoralty of Bordeaux at the baths Della
Villa, near Lucca; but, faithful to his resolution
to have done with " public life," he declined the
honour, and, after a second visit to Rome, returned
slowly into France, with the intention of resuming
the peaceful and studious leisure which his long
wanderings had made doubly sweet to him. He
found, however, that his friends condemned his
inactivity, and that the citizens of Bordeaux were
resolved not to let him off. Finally he consented
—not, however, till the king (Henri III.) had

interposed his authority—and entered on the office in January, 1582. His administration was more than usually capable, and he received the rare honour of re-election for a second term of office. During his mayoralty, and after it, he was engaged, on more than one occasion, in transactions of public importance. The history of these, as it has been laboriously pieced together out of the correspondence, acts, registers, and other remains of the time, will be gone through with interest by the circumstantial student. The general reader may perhaps be satisfied with a summary remark upon them. All the negotiations in which Montaigne was thus engaged exhibit his character in a light consistent with what we know of him. We see that he was trusted and recognised on all hands as a gentleman of worth, honour, and experience, to whose management and discretion men were glad to entrust their interests in critical cases. In a time of general suspicion, during protracted civil and religious warfare which had proved a "veritable school of treachery and dissimulation," the open, loyal, straightforward conduct of Montaigne gained him the confidence of both parties. But we do not see him engaged, or ambitious to be engaged, in strictly state affairs, or the more momentous crises of the difficult politics of that shifting scene. His character, wanting in energy and ambition, did not supply the defect of birth, which had not placed him among " les grands." He was not qualified, and did not affect, to lead. Any expectation that he should have taken a prominent part in the transactions of his time arises in us from our looking back to his life through the halo of his after-fame. We think that so much worldly wisdom and solid sense must have made itself felt on the theatre of public affairs. It is sufficiently apparent, notwithstanding M. Grün's violent efforts to drag him forward, that Montaigne's indolent and meditative temperament kept him remote from the turmoil of public life. That he was in any degree forced into active duties is to be ascribed to the same easy disposition. He allowed his friends to impose labours which he would never have assumed. " Je ne me mets point hors de moi." " Il faut se prêter à autrui, et ne se donner qu'à soi meme." These are his characteristic maxims. He is no Hamlet, however. When action is thrust upon him, he is vigilant, steady, and efficient in its performance.

Nothing, in fact, can be less logical than to allow the splendid fame that has gathered round the *Essais* to react on our conceptions of their author's life. It would be a very vulgar inference that one who has left us a great book must have done great things. No one, indeed, would seriously argue thus, but such a feeling may insensibly influence the expectation we form. The title of the work before us, *La Vie Publique de Montaigne*, appears as if it were a response to this illusory anticipation. It can only lead to disappointment. As the life of a private country gentleman, loved by his friends, respected by his enemies, trusted by all, and of

I   33   D

whom all regretted that he shunned employment,
it corresponds perfectly to the careless wisdom
and unaffected sagacity of his written page. To
attempt to pass him off as a public man only leads
a reader to the mortifying exclamation, " Is this
all? " Montaigne, stripped of the essayist, looks
to us as he did to the courtiers of his own time.
How, Brantôme will witness:

In our time we have seen lawyers issue from the
courts, throw aside the cap and gown, and take to
wearing the sword. We have seen those, I say, get
the collar of St. Michael without having served at
all. Thus did the Sieur de Montaigne, who had far
better have stuck to his pen and gone on scribbling
essays, than changed it for a sword, which did not
sit so well on him. Doubtless his kinsman, the
Marquis de Trans, got him knighted by the king,
in order to turn the order into ridicule, for the
marquis was always a great mocker.[1]

Such was Montaigne to the courtiers of his own
day. The essayist has indeed had his revenge!
The growth of his fame, however, has not been
continuous. During his own lifetime, and for some
time after his death, it was steadily on the increase.
He himself saw five editions of his *Essais* through
the press, and thirty-one editions have been counted
between 1580 and 1650. There were very soon
two complete translations into English, and, through
Shakespeare's use of Florio's version, the blood of
Montaigne may be said to have flowed into the
very veins of our literature. Pascal had studied
him till he almost knew him by heart. But as the

[1] *Capitaines Illustres*, art. " Tavanne."

growth of the *Siècle* literature gave a new direction
to thought and taste, the credit of Montaigne
declined. It was not without difficulty that he was
admitted among the authorities of the Dictionary
of the Academy. Bossuet only names him once, and
then he is " un Montaigne." Fénelon mentions
him, but it is to reproach him with his Gascon
words. And it is a significant fact that from 1669
to 1724 not a single edition of the *Essais* was called
for. Later times have made abundant atonement
for this temporary neglect. Few other books of
the sixteenth century could be named which issue
from the press at the rate of one edition a year.
The original editions sell at bibliomaniac prices.
The *Cæsar*, with his autograph, for which M.
Parison gave eighteen sous, was knocked down to
the Duc d'Aumale at 1550 francs. Of late years
especially, an amount of industry has been expended
in elucidating his life and writings such as is only
devoted to the great classics of a language. We
believe that all his fellow-labourers will agree in
assigning to Dr. Payen precedence in their joint
efforts. His name, like that of Mademoiselle de
Gournay, must ever be associated with that of
Montaigne. But investigation is still in progress.
It is far from complete. It has not arrived at
that stage, nor have its results been yet sufficiently sifted to allow such a biography of Montaigne to be written as will last, and we must
regard M. Grün's volume as a temporary and
only partial substitute.

A WORD ABOUT SPINOZA

By Matthew Arnold

' By the sentence of the angels, by the decree of
the saints, we anathematise, cut off, curse, and
execrate Baruch Spinoza, in the presence of these
sacred books with the six hundred and thirteen
precepts which are written therein, with the
anathema wherewith Joshua anathematised Jericho;
with the cursing wherewith Elisha cursed the
children; and with all the cursings which are
written in the Book of the Law: cursed be he by
day, and cursed by night; cursed when he lieth
down, and cursed when he riseth up; cursed when
he goeth out, and cursed when he cometh in; the
Lord pardon him never; the wrath and fury of
the Lord burn upon this man, and bring upon him
all the curses which are written in the Book of the
Law. The Lord blot out his name under heaven.
The Lord set him apart for destruction from all
the tribes of Israel, with all the curses of the firma-
ment which are written in the Book of this Law.
. . . There shall no man speak to him, no man
write to him, no man show him any kindness, no
man stay under the same roof with him, no man
come nigh him."

With these amenities, the current compliments of theological parting, the Jews of the Portuguese synagogue at Amsterdam took in 1656 (and not in 1660, as has till now been commonly supposed) their leave of their erring brother, Baruch or Benedict Spinoza. They remained children of Israel, and he became a child of modern Europe.

That was in 1656, and Spinoza died in 1677, at the early age of forty-four. Glory had not found him out. His short life—a life of unbroken diligence, kindliness, and purity—was passed in seclusion. But in spite of that seclusion, in spite of the shortness of his career, in spite of the hostility of the dispensers of renown in the eighteenth century,—of Voltaire's disparagement and Bayle's detraction,—in spite of the repellent form which he has given to his principal work, in spite of the exterior semblance of a rigid dogmatism alien to the most essential tendencies of modern philosophy, in spite, finally, of the immense weight of disfavour cast upon him by the long-repeated charge of atheism, Spinoza's name has silently risen in importance, the man and his work have attracted a steadily increasing notice, and bid fair to become soon what they deserve to become,—in the history of modern philosophy, the central point of interest. An avowed translation of one of his works,—his *Tractatus Theologico-Politicus* of which I spoke here some months ago,—has at last made its appearance in English. It is the principal work which Spinoza published in his lifetime; his book on ethics, the work on which his fame rests, is posthumous.

The English translator has not done his task well. Of the character of his version there can, I am afraid, be no doubt; one such passage as the following is decisive:

" I confess that, *while with them* (the theologians) *I have never been able sufficiently to admire the unfathomed mysteries of Scripture, I have still found them giving utterance to nothing but Aristotelian and Platonic speculations,* artfully dressed up and cunningly accommodated to Holy Writ, lest the speakers should show themselves too plainly to belong to the sect of the Grecian heathens. *Nor was it enough for these men to discourse with the Greeks, they have further taken to raving with the Hebrew prophets.*"

This professes to be a translation of these words of Spinoza: " Fateor, eos nunquam satis mirari potuisse Scripturæ profundissima mysteria; attamen præter Aristotelicorum vel Platonicorum speculationes nihil docuisse video, atque his, ne gentiles sectari viderentur, Scripturam accommodaverunt. Non satis his fuit cum Graecis insanire, sed prophetas cum iisdem deliravisse voluerunt." After one such specimen of a translator's force, the experienced reader has a sort of instinct that he may as well close the book at once, with a smile or a sigh, according as he happens to be a follower of the weeping or of the laughing philosopher. If, in spite of this instinct, he persists in going on with the English version of the *Tractatus Theologico-Politicus*, he will find many more such specimens. It is not, however, my intention to fill my space with these, or with strictures upon their author. I prefer to remark, that he renders a service to literary history by pointing out, in his preface, how " to Bayle may be traced the disfavour in which the name of Spinoza was so long held "; that, in his observations on the system of the Church of England, he shows a laudable freedom from the prejudices of ordinary English Liberals of that advanced school to which he clearly belongs; and lastly, that, though he manifests little familiarity with Latin, he seems to have considerable familiarity with philosophy, and to be well able to follow and comprehend speculative reasoning. Let me advise him to unite his forces with those of some one who has that accurate knowledge of Latin which he himself has not, and then, perhaps, of that union a really good translation of Spinoza will be the result. And, having given him this advice, let me again return, for a little, to the *Tractatus Theologico-Politicus* itself.

This work, as I have already said, is a work on the interpretation of Scripture—it treats of the Bible. What was it exactly which Spinoza thought about the Bible and its inspiration? That will be, at the present moment, the central point of interest for the English readers of his Treatise. Now I wish to observe—what it was irrelevant to my purpose to observe when I before spoke of the

Tractatus Theologico-Politicus—that just on this very point the Treatise, interesting and remarkable as it is, will fail to satisfy the reader. It is important to seize this notion quite firmly, and not to quit hold of it while one is reading Spinoza's work. The scope of that work is this. Spinoza sees that the life and practice of Christian nations professing the religion of the Bible, are not the due fruits of the religion of the Bible; he sees only hatred, bitterness, and strife, where he might have expected to see love, joy, and peace in believing; and he asks himself the reason of this. The reason is, he says, that these people misunderstand their Bible. Well, then, is his conclusion, I will write a *Tractatus Theologico-Politicus*. I will show these people, that, taking the Bible for granted, taking it to be all which it asserts itself to be, taking it to have all the authority which it claims, it is not what they imagine it to be, it does not say what they imagine it to say. I will show them what it really does say, and I will show them that they will do well to accept this real teaching of the Bible, instead of the phantom with which they have so long been cheated. I will show their Governments that they will do well to remodel the National Churches, to make of them institutions informed with the spirit of the true Bible, instead of institutions informed with the spirit of this false phantom.

Such is really the scope of Spinoza's work. He pursues a great object, and pursues it with signal ability; but it is important to observe that he does not give us his own opinion about the Bible's fundamental character. He takes the Bible as it stands, as he might take the phenomena of nature, and he discusses it as he finds it. Revelation differs from natural knowledge, he says, not by being more divine or more certain than natural knowledge, but by being conveyed in a different way; it differs from it because it is a knowledge " of which the laws of human nature considered in themselves alone cannot be the cause." What is really its cause, he says, we need not here inquire (*verum nec nobis jam opus est propheticæ cognitionis causam scire*), for we take Scripture, which contains this revelation, as it stands, and do not ask how it arose (*documentorum causas nihil curamus*).

Proceeding on this principle, Spinoza leaves the attentive reader somewhat baffled and disappointed, clear as is his way of treating his subject, and remarkable as are the conclusions with which he presents us. He starts, we feel, from what is to him a hypothesis, and we want to know what he really thinks about this hypothesis. His greatest novelties are all within limits fixed for him by this hypothesis. He says that the voice which called Samuel was an imaginary voice; he says that the waters of the Red Sea retreated before a strong wind; he says that the Shunammite's son was revived by the natural heat of Elisha's body; he says that the rainbow which was made a sign to Noah appeared in the ordinary course of nature. Scripture itself, rightly interpreted, says, he affirms, all this. But he asserts

that the Voice which uttered the commandments
on Mount Sinai was a real voice, a *vera vox*. He
says, indeed, that this voice could not really give
to the Israelites that proof which they imagined
it gave to them of the existence of God, and that
God on Sinai was dealing with the Israelites only
according to their imperfect knowledge. Still he
asserts the voice to have been a real one; and for
this reason, that we do violence to Scripture if we
do not admit it to have been a real one (*nisi Scripturæ
vim inferre velimus, omnino concedendum est, Israëlitas
veram vocem audivisse*). The attentive reader wants
to know what Spinoza himself thought about this
vera vox and its possibility; he is much more interested in knowing this than in knowing what Spinoza
considered Scripture to affirm about the matter.

The feeling of perplexity thus caused is not
diminished by the language of the chapter on
miracles. In this chapter Spinoza broadly affirms
a miracle to be an impossibility. But he himself
contrasts the method of demonstration *a priori*, by
which he claims to have established this proposition,
with the method which he has pursued in treating
of prophetic revelation. "This revelation," he
says, "is a matter out of human reach, and therefore I was bound to take it as I found it." *Monere
volo, me aliâ prorsus methodo circa miracula pro-
cessisse, quam circa prophetiam . . . quod etiam
consulto feci, quia de prophetiâ, quandoquidem ipsa
captum humanum superat et quæstio mere theologica
est, nihil affirmare, neque etiam scire poteram in*

quo ipsa potissimum constiterit, nisi ex fundamentis revelatis. The reader feels that Spinoza, proceeding on a hypothesis, has presented him with the assertion of a miracle, and afterwards, proceeding *a priori*, has presented him with the assertion that a miracle is impossible. He feels that Spinoza does not adequately reconcile these two assertions by declaring that any event really miraculous, if found recorded in Scripture, must be " a spurious addition made to Scripture by sacrilegious men." Is, then, he asks, the *vera vox* of Mount Sinai in Spinoza's opinion a spurious addition made to Scripture by sacrilegious men; or, if not, how is it not miraculous?

Spinoza, in his own mind, regarded the Bible as a vast collection of miscellaneous documents, many of them quite disparate and not at all to be harmonised with others; documents of unequal value and of varying applicability, some of them conveying ideas salutary for one time, others for another. But in the *Tractatus Theologico-Politicus* he by no means always deals in this free spirit with the Bible. Sometimes he chooses to deal with it in the spirit of the veriest worshipper of the letter; sometimes he chooses to treat the Bible as if all its parts were (so to speak) equipollent; to snatch an isolated text which suits his purpose, without caring whether it is annulled by the context, by the general drift of Scripture, or by other passages of more weight and authority. The great critic thus voluntarily becomes as uncritical as Exeter Hall. The epicurean Solomon, whose *Ecclesiastes* the Hebrew doctors,

even after they had received it into the canon,
forbade the young and weak-minded among their
community to read, Spinoza quotes as of the same
authority with the severe Moses; he uses promis-
cuously, as documents of identical force, without
discriminating between their essentially different
character, the softened cosmopolitan teaching of
the prophets of the captivity and the rigid national
teaching of the instructors of Israel's youth. He is
capable of extracting, from a chance expression of
Jeremiah, the assertion of a speculative idea which
Jeremiah certainly never entertained, and from
which he would have recoiled in dismay,—the
idea, namely, that miracles are impossible; just
as the ordinary Englishman can extract from God's
words to Noah, *Be fruitful and multiply*, an ex-
hortation to himself to have a large family. Spinoza,
I repeat, knew perfectly well what this verbal
mode of dealing with the Bible was worth: but
he sometimes uses it because of the hypothesis
from which he set out; because of his having
agreed " to take Scripture as it stands, and not to
ask how it arose."

No doubt the sagacity of Spinoza's rules for
biblical interpretation, the power of his analysis
of the contents of the Bible, the interest of his
reflections on Jewish history, are, in spite of this,
very great, and have an absolute worth of their
own, independent of the silence or ambiguity of
their author upon a point of cardinal importance.
Few candid people will read his rules of inter-

pretation without exclaiming that they are the very
dictates of good sense, that they have always believed in them; and without adding, after a moment's
reflection, that they have passed their lives in
violating them. And what can be more interesting,
than to find that perhaps the main cause of the
decay of the Jewish polity was one of which from
our English Bible, which entirely mistranslates
the 26th verse of the 20th chapter of Ezekiel, we
hear nothing,—the perpetual reproach of impurity
and rejection cast upon the mass of the Hebrew
nation by the exclusive priesthood of the tribe of
Levi? What can be more suggestive, after Mr.
Mill and Dr. Stanley have been telling us how great
an element of strength to the Hebrew nation was
the institution of prophets, than to hear from the
ablest of Hebrews how this institution seems to
him to have been to his nation one of her main
elements of weakness? No intelligent man can
read the *Tractatus Theologico-Politicus* without
being profoundly instructed by it: but neither can
he read it without feeling that, as a speculative
work, it is, to use a French military expression, *in
the air*; that, in a certain sense, it is in want of a
base and in want of supports; that this base and
these supports are, at any rate, not to be found in
the work itself, and, if they exist, must be sought
for in other works of the author.

The genuine speculative opinions of Spinoza,
which the *Tractatus Theologico-Politicus* but imperfectly reveals, may in his *Ethics* and in his

Letters be found set forth clearly. It is, however, the business of criticism to deal with every independent work as with an independent whole, and —instead of establishing between the *Tractatus Theologico-Politicus* and the *Ethics* of Spinoza a relation which Spinoza himself has not established, —to seize, in dealing with the *Tractatus Theologico-Politicus*, the important fact that this work has its source, not in the axioms and definitions of the *Ethics*, but in a hypothesis. The *Ethics* are not yet translated into English, and I have not here to speak of them. Then will be the right time for criticism to try and seize the special character and tendencies of that remarkable work, when it is dealing with it directly. The criticism of the *Ethics* is far too serious a task to be undertaken incidentally, and merely as a supplement to the criticism of the *Tractatus Theologico-Politicus*. Nevertheless, on certain governing ideas of Spinoza, which receive their systematic expression, indeed, in the *Ethics*, and on which the *Tractatus Theologico-Politicus* is not formally based, but which are yet never absent from Spinoza's mind in the composition of any work, which breathe through all his works, and fill them with a peculiar effect and power, I wish before concluding these remarks, to say a few words.

A philosopher's real power over mankind resides not in his metaphysical formulas, but in the spirit and tendencies which have led him to adopt those formulas. Spinoza's critic, therefore, has rather to bring to light that spirit and those tendencies of his author, than to exhibit his metaphysical formulas. Propositions about substance pass by mankind at large like the idle wind, which mankind at large regards not; it will not even listen to a word about these propositions, unless it first learns what their author was driving at with them, and finds that this object of his is one with which it sympathises, one, at any rate, which commands its attention. And mankind is so far right that this object of the author is really, as has been said, that which is most important, that which sets all his work in motion, that which is the secret of his attraction for other minds, which, by different ways, pursue the same object.

Mr. Maurice, seeking for the cause of Goethe's great admiration for Spinoza, thinks that he finds it in Spinoza's Hebrew genius. " He spoke of God," says Mr. Maurice, " as an actual being, to those who had fancied him a name in a book. The child of the circumcision had a message for Lessing and Goethe which the pagan schools of philosophy could not bring." This seems to me, I confess, fanciful. An intensity and impressiveness, which came to him from his Hebrew nature, Spinoza no doubt has; but the two things which are most remarkable about him, and by which, as I think, he chiefly impressed Goethe, seem to me not to come to him from his Hebrew nature at all,—I mean his denial of final causes, and his stoicism, a stoicism not passive, but active. For a mind like Goethe's, — a mind profoundly impartial and

MATTHEW ARNOLD

passionately aspiring after the science, not of men only, but of universal nature,—the popular philosophy which explains all things by reference to man, and regards universal nature as existing for the sake of man, and even of certain classes of men, was utterly repulsive. Unchecked, this philosophy would gladly maintain that the donkey exists in order that the invalid Christian may have donkey's milk before breakfast; and such views of nature as this were exactly what Goethe's whole soul abhorred. Creation, he thought, should be made of sterner stuff; he desired to rest the donkey's existence on larger grounds. More than any philosopher who has ever lived, Spinoza satisfied him here. The full exposition of the counter-doctrine to the popular doctrine of final causes is to be found in the Ethics; but this denial of final causes was so essential an element of all Spinoza's thinking that we shall, as has been said already, find in it the work with which we are here concerned, the *Tractatus Theologico-Politicus*, and, indeed, permeating that work and all his works. From the *Tractatus Theologico-Politicus* one may take as good a general statement of this denial as any which is to be found in the *Ethics*:

" Deus naturam dirigit, prout ejus leges universales, non autem prout humanæ naturæ particulares leges exigunt, adeoque Deus non solius humani generis, sed totius naturæ rationem habet. (*God directs nature, according as the universal laws of nature, but not according as the particular laws of*

48

*human nature require; and so God has regard, not
of the human race only, but of entire nature.)*"

And, as a pendant to this denial by Spinoza of
final causes, comes his stoicism:

"Non studemus, ut natura nobis, sed contra
ut nos naturæ pareamus. (*Our desire is not that
nature may obey us, but, on the contrary that we may
obey nature.*)"

Here is the second source of his attractiveness
for Goethe; and Goethe is but the eminent representative of a whole order of minds whose admiration has made Spinoza's fame. Spinoza first
impresses Goethe and any man like Goethe, and
then he composes him; first he fills and satisfies his
imagination by the width and grandeur of his view
of nature, and then he fortifies and stills his mobile,
straining, passionate poetic temperament by the
moral lesson he draws from his view of nature.
And a moral lesson not of mere resigned acquiescence, not of melancholy quietism, but of joyful
activity within the limits of man's true sphere:

"Ipsa hominis essentia est conatus quo unus-
quisque suum esse conservare conatur. . . . Virtus
hominis est ipsa hominis essentia, quatenus a solo
conatu suum esse conservandi definitur. . .
Felicitas in eo consistit quod homo suum esse
conservare potest. . . . Lætitia est hominis transitio ad majorem perfectionem. . . . Tristitia est
hominis transitio ad minorem perfectionem. (*Man's
very essence is the effort wherewith each man strives
to maintain his own being. . . . Man's virtue is*

I   49   E

this very essence, so far as it is defined by this single effort to maintain his own being. . . . Happiness consists in a man's being able to maintain his own being. . . . Joy is man's passage to a greater perfection. . . . Sorrow is man's passage to a lesser perfection.)"

It seems to me that by neither of these, his grand characteristic doctrines, is Spinoza truly Hebrew or truly Christian. His denial of final causes is essentially alien to the spirit of the Old Testament, and his cheerful and self-sufficing stoicism is essentially alien to the spirit of the New. The doctrine that "God directs nature, not according as the particular laws of human nature, but according as the universal laws of nature require," is at utter variance with that Hebrew mode of representing God's dealings, which makes the locusts visit Egypt to punish Pharaoh's hardness of heart, and the falling dew avert itself from the fleece of Gideon. The doctrine that "all sorrow is a passage to a lesser perfection" is at utter variance with the Christian recognition of the blessedness of sorrow, working "repentance to salvation not to be repented of"; of sorrow, which, in Dante's words, "remarries us to God." Spinoza's repeated and earnest assertions that the love of God is man's *summum bonum* do not remove the fundamental diversity between his doctrine and the Hebrew and Christian doctrines. By the love of God he does not mean the same thing as the Hebrew and Christian religions mean by the love of God. He makes the love of God to consist in the knowledge of God; and, as we

SPINOZA

know God only through his manifestation of himself
in the laws of all nature, it is by knowing these
laws that we love God, and the more we know
them the more we love him. This may be true,
but this is not what the Christian means by the love
of God. Spinoza's ideal is the intellectual life; the
Christian's ideal is the religious life. Between the
two states there is all the difference which there
is between the being in love, and the following,
with delighted comprehension, a demonstration of
Euclid. For Spinoza, undoubtedly, the crown
of the intellectual life is a transport, as for the
saint the crown of the religious life is a transport;
but the two transports are not the same.

This is true; yet it is true, also, that by thus
crowning the intellectual life with a sacred transport, by thus retaining in philosophy, amid the
discontented murmurs of all the army of atheism,
the name of God, Spinoza maintains a profound
affinity with that which is truest in religion, and
inspires an indestructible interest. "It is true,"
one may say to the wise and devout Christian,
"Spinoza's conception of beatitude is not yours,
and cannot satisfy you, but whose conception of
beatitude would you accept as satisfying? Not
even that of the devoutest of your fellow-Christians.
Fra Angelico, the sweetest and most inspired of
devout souls, has given us, in his great picture of
the Last Judgment, his conception of beatitude.
The elect are going round in a ring on long grass
under laden fruit-trees; two of them, more restless

than the others, are flying up a battlemented street,
—a street blank with all the ennui of the Middle
Ages. Across a gulf is visible, for the delectation
of the saints, a blazing caldron in which Beelzebub
is sousing the damned. This is hardly more your
conception of beatitude than Spinoza's is. But
'in my Father's house are many mansions'; only,
to reach any one of these mansions, are needed
the wings of a genuine sacred transport, of an
'immortal longing.'" These wings Spinoza had;
and, because he had them he horrifies a certain
school of his admirers by talking of "God" where
they talk of "forces," and by talking of "the love
of God" where they talk of "a rational curiosity."

One of his admirers, M. Van Vloten, has recently published at Amsterdam a supplementary
volume to Spinoza's works, containing the interesting document of Spinoza's sentence of excom-
munication, from which I have already quoted,
and containing, besides, several lately found works
alleged to be Spinoza's, which seem to me to be
of doubtful authenticity, and, even if authentic,
of no great importance. M. Van Vloten (who,
let me be permitted to say in passing, writes a Latin
which would make one think that the art of writing
Latin must be now a lost art in the country of
Lipsius) is very anxious that Spinoza's unscien-
tific retention of the name of God should not
afflict his readers with any doubts as to his perfect
scientific orthodoxy:

"It is a great mistake," he cries, "to disparage

Spinoza as merely one of the dogmatists before Kant. By keeping the name of God, while he did away with his person and character, he has done himself injustice. Those who look to the bottom of things will see, that, long ago as he lived, he had even then reached the point to which the post-Hegelian philosophy and the study of natural science has only just brought our own times. Leibnitz expressed his apprehension lest those who did away with final causes should do away with God at the same time. But it is in his having done away with final causes, *and with God along with them*, that Spinoza's true merit consists."

Now it must be remarked that to use Spinoza's denial of final causes in order to identify him with the Coryphæi of atheism, is to make a false use of Spinoza's denial of final causes, just as to use his assertion of the all-importance of loving God to identify him with the saints would be to make a false use of his assertion of the all-importance of loving God. He is no more to be identified with the post-Hegelian philosophers than he is to be identified with St. Augustine. Nay, when M. Van Vloten violently presses the parallel with the post-Hegelians, one feels that the parallel with St. Augustine is the far truer one. Compared with the soldier of irreligion M. Van Vloten would have him to be, Spinoza is religious. His own language about himself, about his aspirations and his course, are true; his foot is in the *vera vita*, his eye on the beatific vision.

A SENSITIVE AGITATOR
(RICHARD COBDEN)

By Walter Bagehot

Twenty-three years ago—and it is very strange that it should be so many years—when Mr. Cobden first began to hold Free-trade meetings in the agricultural districts, people there were much confused. They could not believe the Mr. Cobden they saw to be the " Mr. Cobden that was in the papers." They expected a burly demagogue from the North, ignorant of rural matters, absorbed in manufacturing ideas, appealing to class prejudices —hostile and exciting hostility. They saw a "sensitive and almost slender man, of shrinking nerve, full of rural ideas, who proclaimed himself the son of a farmer, who understood and could state the facts of agricultural life far better than most agriculturists, who was most anxious to convince every one of what he thought the truth, and who was almost more anxious not to offend any one." The tradition is dying out, but Mr. Cobden acquired, even in those days of Free-trade agitation, a sort of agricultural popularity. He excited a personal interest, he left what may be called a *sense* of himself among his professed enemies. They were surprised at finding that he was not what they thought; they were charmed to find that he was not what they expected; they were fascinated to find what he was. The same feeling has been evident at his sudden death—a death at least which was to the mass of occupied men sudden. Over political Belgravia—the last part of English society Mr. Cobden ever cultivated—there was a sadness. Every one felt that England had lost an individuality which it could never have again, which was of the highest value, which was in its own kind altogether unequalled.

What used to strike the agricultural mind, as different from what they fancied, and most opposite to a Northern agitator, was a sort of playfulness. They could hardly believe that the lurking smile, the perfectly magical humour which they were so much struck by, could be that of a " Manchester man." Mr. Cobden used to say, " I have as much right as any man to call myself the representative of the tenant farmer, for I am a farmer's son, and the son of a Sussex farmer." But agriculturists keenly felt that this was not the explanation of the man they saw. Perhaps they could not have thoroughly explained, but they perfectly knew that they were hearing a man of singular and most peculiar genius, fitted as if by " natural selection " for the work he had to do, and not wasting a word on any other work or anything else, least of all upon himself.

Mr. Cobden was very anomalous in two respects.
He was a sensitive agitator. Generally, an agitator
is a rough man of the O'Connell type, who says
anything himself, and lets others say anything.
You "peg into me and I will peg into you, and let
us see which will win," is his motto. But Mr.
Cobden's habit and feeling were utterly different.
He never spoke ill of any one. He arraigned
principles, but not persons. We fearlessly say that
after a career of agitation of thirty years, not one
single individual has—we do not say a valid charge,
but a producible charge—a charge which he would
wish to bring forward against Mr. Cobden. You
cannot find the man who says, " Mr. Cobden said
this of me, and it was not true." This may seem
trivial praise, and on paper it looks easy. But to
those who know the great temptations of actual
life it means very much. How would any other
great agitator, O'Connell or Hunt or Cobbett look,
if tried by such a test? Very rarely, if even ever
in history, has a man achieved so much by his
words—been victor in what was thought at the
time to be a class struggle—and yet spoken so little
evil as Mr. Cobden. There is hardly a word to
be found, perhaps, even now, which the recording
angel would wish to blot out. We may on other
grounds object to an agitator who lacerates no one,
but no watchful man of the world will deny that
such an agitator has vanquished one of life's most
imperious and difficult temptations.

Perhaps some of our readers may remember

as vividly as we do a curious instance of Mr. Cobden's sensitiveness. He said at Drury Lane Theatre, in tones of feeling, almost of passion, curiously contrasting with the ordinary coolness of his nature, " I could not serve with Sir Robert Peel." After more than twenty years, the curiously thrilling tones of that phrase still live in our ears. Mr. Cobden alluded to the charge which Sir Robert Peel had made, or half made, that the Anti-Corn Law League and Mr. Cobden had, by their action and agitation, conduced to the actual assassination of Mr. Drummond, his secretary, and the intended assassination of himself—Sir Robert Peel. No excuse or palliation could be made for such an assertion except the most important one, that Peel's nerves were as susceptible and sensitive as Mr. Cobden's. But the profound feeling with which Mr. Cobden spoke of it is certain. He felt it as a man feels an unjust calumny, an unfounded stain on his honour.

Mr. Disraeli said on one occasion (and he has made many extraordinary assertions, but this is about the queerest), " Mr. Cobden had a profound reverence for tradition." If there is any single quality which Mr. Cobden had not, it was traditional reverence. But probably Mr. Disraeli meant what was most true, that Mr. Cobden had a delicate dislike of offending other men's opinions. He dealt with them tenderly. He did not like to have his own creed coarsely attacked, and he did—he could not help doing—as he would be done by; he never attacked any man's creed coarsely or roughly, or in any way except by what he in his best conscience thought the fairest and justest argument.

This sensitive nature is one marked peculiarity in Mr. Cobden's career as an agitator, and another is, that he was an agitator for men of business.

Generally speaking, occupied men charged with the responsibilities and laden with the labour of grave affairs are jealous of agitation. They know how much may be said against any one who is responsible for anything. They know how unanswerable such charges nearly always are, and how false they easily may be. A capitalist can hardly help thinking, "Suppose a man was to make a speech against my mode of conducting my own business, how much he would have to say!" Now it is an exact description of Mr. Cobden, that by the personal magic of a single-minded practicability he made men of business abandon this objection. He made them rather like the new form of agitation. He made them say, " How business-like, how wise, just what it would have been right to do."

Mr. Cobden of course was not the discoverer of the Free-trade principle. He did not first find out that the Corn Laws were bad laws. But he was the most effectual of those who discovered how the Corn Laws were to be repealed, how Free-trade was to change from a doctrine of the *Wealth of Nations* into a principle of tariffs and a fact of real life. If a thing was right, to Mr. Cobden's mind it ought to be done; and as Adam

Smith's doctrines were admitted on theory, he could not believe that they ought to lie idle, that they ought to be "bedridden in the dormitory of the understanding."

Lord Houghton once said, "In my time political economy books used to begin, 'Suppose a man on an island.'" Mr. Cobden's speeches never began so. He was altogether a man of business speaking to men of business. Some of us may remember the almost arch smile with which he said, "The House of Commons does not seem quite to understand the difference between a cotton mill and a print work." It was almost amusing to him to think that the first assembly of the first mercantile nation could be, as they were and are, very dim in their notions of the most material divisions of their largest industry. It was this evident and first-hand familiarity with real facts and actual life which enabled Mr. Cobden to inspire a curiously diffused confidence in all matter-of-fact men. He diffused a kind of "economical faith." People in those days had only to say, "Mr. Cobden said so," and other people went and "believed it."

Mr. Cobden had nothing in the received sense classical about his oratory, but it is quite certain that Aristotle, the greatest teacher of the classical art of rhetoric, would very keenly have appreciated his oratory. This sort of economical faith is exactly what he would most have valued, what he most prescribed. He said: "A speaker should convince his audience that he was a likely person to know."

This was exactly what Mr. Cobden did. And the matter-of-fact philosopher would have much liked Mr. Cobden's habit of "coming to the point." It would have been thoroughly agreeable to his positive mind to see so much of clear, obvious argument. He would not, indeed, have been able to conceive a "League Meeting." There has never, perhaps, been another time in the history of the world when excited masses of men and women hung on the words of one talking political economy. The excitement of these meetings was keener than any political excitement of the last twenty years, keener infinitely than any which there is now. It may be said, and truly, that the interest of the subject was Mr. Cobden's felicity, not his mind; but it may be said with equal truth that the excitement was much greater when he was speaking than when any one else was speaking. By a kind of keenness of nerve, he said the exact word most fitted to touch, not the bare abstract understanding, but the quick individual perceptions of his hearers.

We do not wish to make this article a mere panegyric. Mr. Cobden was far too manly to like such folly. His mind was very peculiar, and like all peculiar minds had its sharp limits. He had what we may call a supplementary understanding, that is, a bold, original intellect, acting on a special experience, and striking out views and principles not known to or neglected by ordinary men. He did not possess the traditional education of his country, and did not understand it. The solid heritage of transmitted knowledge has more value, we believe, than he would have accorded to it. There was too a defect in business faculty not identical, but perhaps not altogether without analogy. The late Mr. James Wilson used to say, " Cobden's administrative power I do not think much of, but he is most valuable in counsel, always original, always shrewd, and not at all extreme." He was not altogether equal to meaner men in some beaten tracks and pathways of life, though he was far their superior in all matters requiring an original stress of speculation, an innate energy of thought.

It may be said, and truly said, that he has been cut off before his time. A youth and manhood so spent as his well deserved a green old age. But so it was not to be. He has left us, quite independently of his positive works, of the repeal of the Corn Laws, of the French treaty, a rare gift—the gift of a unique character. There has been nothing before Richard Cobden like him in English history, and perhaps there will not be anything like him. And his character is of the simple, emphatic, pic-turesque sort which most easily, when opportunities are given as they were to him, goes down to posterity. May posterity learn from him! Only last week we hoped to have learned something ourselves.

> But what is before us we know not,
>   And we know not what shall succeed.

"A CHARM OF BIRDS" [1]

By Charles Kingsley

Is it merely a fancy that we English, the educated
people among us at least, are losing that love for
spring which among our old forefathers rose almost
to worship? That the perpetual miracle of the bud-
ding leaves and the returning song-birds awakes no
longer in us the astonishment which it awoke yearly
among the dwellers in the old world, when the sun
was a god who was sick to death each winter, and
returned in spring to life and health, and glory;
when the death of Adonis, at the autumnal equinox,
was wept over by the Syrian women, and the death
of Baldur, in the colder north, by all living things,
even to the dripping trees, and the rocks furrowed
by the autumn rains; when Freya, the goddess of
youth and love, went forth over the earth each
spring, while the flowers broke forth under her
tread over the brown moors, and the birds welcomed
her with song; when, according to Olaus Magnus,
the Goths and South Swedes had, on the return of
spring, a mock battle between summer and winter,
and welcomed the returning splendour of the sun
with dancing and mutual feasting, rejoicing that a

[1] *Fraser's Magazine,* June 1867.

better season for fishing and hunting was approaching? To those simpler children of a simpler age, in more direct contact with the daily and yearly facts of Nature, and more dependent on them for their bodily food and life, winter and spring were the two great facts of existence; the symbols, the one of death, the other of life; and the battle between the two—the battle of the sun with darkness, of winter with spring, of death with life, of bereavement with love—lay at the root of all their myths and all their creeds. Surely a change has come over our fancies. The seasons are little to us now. We are nearly as comfortable in winter as in summer, or in spring. Nay, we have begun, of late, to grumble at the two latter as much as at the former, and talk (and not without excuse at times) of "the treacherous month of May," and of "summer having set in with its usual severity." We work for the most part in cities and towns, and the seasons pass by us unheeded. May and June are spent by most educated people anywhere rather than among birds and flowers. They do not escape into the country till the elm hedges are growing black, and the song-birds silent, and the hay cut, and all the virgin bloom of the country has passed into a sober and matronly ripeness—if not into the sere and yellow leaf. Our very landscape painters, till Creswick arose and recalled to their minds the fact that trees were sometimes green, were wont to paint few but brown autumnal scenes. As for the song of birds, of which in the middle age no

poet could say enough, our modern poets seem to
be forgetting that birds ever sing.

It was not so of old. The climate, perhaps, was
more severe than now; the transition from winter
to spring more sudden, like that of Scandinavia
now. Clearage of forests and drainage of land have
equalised our seasons, or rather made them more
uncertain. More broken winters are followed by
more broken springs; and May-day is no longer a
marked point to be kept as a festival by all child-
like hearts. The merry month of May is merry
only in stage songs. The May garlands and dances
are all but gone: the borrowed plate, and the
milkmaids who borrowed it, gone utterly. No
more does Mrs. Pepys go to lie at Woolwich,
" in order to a little ayre and to gather Maydew "
for her complexion, by Mrs. Turner's advice. The
Maypole is gone likewise; and never more shall
the puritan soul of a Stubbs be aroused in indignation at seeing " against Maie, every parish, towne,
and village assemble themselves together, both men,
women, and children, olde and young, all indif-
ferently, and goe into the woodes and groves,
hilles and mountaines, where they spend the night
in pastyme, and in the morning they returne,
bringing with them birch bowes and braunches of
trees to deck their assembly withal. . . . They
have twentie or fourtie yoke of oxen, every oxe
having a sweete nosegay of flowers tyed on the
tippe of his hornes, and these draw home this Maypole (this stincking idol rather) which is covered all

over with flowers and hearbes, with two or three hundred men, women, and children following it with great devotion. . . . And then they fall to banquet and feast, daunce and leap about it, as the heathen people did at the dedication of their idolles, whereof this is a perfect pattern, or the thing itself."

This, and much more, says poor Stubbs, in his *Anatomie of Abuses*, and had, no doubt, good reason enough for his virtuous indignation at May-day scandals. But people may be made dull without being made good; and the direct and only effect of putting down May games and such like was to cut off the dwellers in towns from all healthy communion with Nature, and leave them to mere sottishness and brutality.

Yet perhaps the May games died out partly because the feelings which had given rise to them died out before improved personal comforts. Of old, men and women fared hardly, and slept cold; and were thankful to Almighty God for every beam of sunshine which roused them out of their long hybernation; thankful for every flower and every bird which reminded them that joy was stronger than sorrow, and life than death. With the spring came not only labour, but enjoyment:

In the spring, the young man's fancy lightly turned to
    thoughts of love,

as lads and lasses, who had been pining for each other by their winter firesides, met again, like Daphnis and Chloe, by shaugh and lea; and learnt

I   65   F to sing from the songs of birds, and to be faithful from their faithfulness.

Then went out troops of fair damsels to seek spring garlands in the forest, as Scheffel has lately sung once more in his "Frau Aventiure"; and, while the dead leaves rattled beneath their feet, hymned "La Regine Avrillouse" to the music of some Minnesinger, whose song was as the song of birds; to whom the birds were friends, fellow-lovers, teachers, mirrors of all which he felt within himself of joyful and tender, true and pure; friends to be fed hereafter (as Walther von der Vogelweide had them fed) with crumbs upon his grave.

True melody, it must be remembered, is un-known, at least at present, in the tropics, and peculiar to the races of those temperate climes into which the song-birds come in spring. It is hard to say why. Exquisite songsters, and those, strangely, of a European type, may be heard any-where in tropical American forests: but native races whose hearts their song can touch are either extinct or yet to come. Some of the old German Minnelieder, on the other hand, seem actually copied from the songs of birds. "Tanderadei" does not merely ask the nightingale to tell no tales; it repeats, in its cadences, the nightingale's song, as the old Minnesinger heard it when he nestled beneath the lime-tree with his love. They are often almost as inarticulate, these old singers, as the birds from whom they copied their notes; the thinnest chain of thought links together some bird-like

refrain: but they make up for their want of logic
and reflection by the depth of their passion, the
perfectness of their harmony with Nature. The
inspired Swabian, wandering in the pine-forest,
listens to the blackbird's voice till it becomes his
own voice; and he breaks out, with the very carol
of the blackbird:

Vogele im Tannenwald pfeifet so hell.
Pfeifet de Wald aus und ein, wo wird mein Schätze sein?
Vogele im Tannenwald pfeifet so hell.

And he has nothing more to say. That is his
whole soul for the time being; and, like a bird,
he sings it over and over again, and never tires.

Another, a Nieder-Rheinischer, watches the
moon rise over the Löwenburg, and thinks upon
his love within the castle hall, till he breaks out
in a strange, sad, tender melody—not without state-
liness and manly confidence in himself and in his
beloved—in the true strain of the nightingale:

Verstohlen geht der Mond auf,
Blau, blau, Blümelein,
Durch Silberwölkchen führt sein Lauf.
Rosen im Thal, Mädel im Saal, O schönste Rosa!

.   .   .   .   .

Und siehst du mich,
Und siehst du sie,
Blau, blau, Blümelein,
Zwei treu're Herzen sah'st du nie;
Rosen im Thalu, . . .

There is little sense in the words, doubtless, according to our modern notions of poetry; but they are

like enough to the long, plaintive notes of the nightingale to say all that the poet has to say, again and again through all his stanzas.

Thus the birds were, to the mediæval singers, their orchestra, or rather their chorus; from the birds they caught their melodies; the sounds which the birds gave them they rendered into words.

And the same bird key-note surely is to be traced in the early English and Scotch songs and ballads, with their often meaningless refrains, sung for the mere pleasure of singing:

> Binnorie, O Binnorie.

Or—

> With a hey lillelu and a how lo lan,
> And the birk and the broom blooms bonnie.

Or—

> She sat down below a thorn,
>   Fine flowers in the valley,
> And there has she her sweet babe born,
>   And the green leaves they grow rarely.

Or even those "fal-la-las," and other nonsense refrains, which, if they were not meant to imitate bird-notes, for what were they meant?

In the old ballads, too, one may hear the bird key-note. He who wrote (and a great rhymer he was)

> As I was walking all alane,
> I heard twa corbies making a mane,

had surely the "mane" of the "corbies" in his ears before it shaped itself into words in his mind:

68

and he had listened to many a "woodwele" who
first thrummed on harp, or fiddled on crowd, how—

> In summer, when the shawes be shene,
>   And leaves be large and long,
> It is full merry in fair forest
>   To hear the fowlés' song.
>
> The wood-wele sang, and wolde not cease,
>   Sitting upon the spray;
> So loud, it wakened Robin Hood
>   In the greenwood where he lay.

And Shakespeare—are not his scraps of song
saturated with these same bird-notes? "Where
the bee sucks," "When daisies pied," "Under the
greenwood tree," "It was a lover and his lass,"
"When daffodils begin to peer," "Ye spotted
snakes," have all a ring in them which was caught
not in the roar of London, or the babble of the
Globe Theatre, but in the woods of Charlecote,
and along the banks of Avon, from

> The ouzel-cock so black of hue,
>   With orange-tawny bill;
> The throstle with his note so true;
>   The wren with little quill;
> The finch, the sparrow, and the lark,
>   The plain-song cuckoo gray—

and all the rest of the birds of the air.

Why is it, again, that so few of our modern
songs are truly songful, and fit to be set to music?
Is it not that the writers of them—persons often
of much taste and poetic imagination—have gone
for their inspiration to the intellect, rather than to

the ear? That (as Shelley does by the skylark, and Wordsworth by the cuckoo), instead of trying to sing like the birds, they only think and talk about the birds, and therefore, however beautiful and true the thoughts and words may be, they are not song? Surely they have not, like the mediæval songsters, studied the speech of the birds, the primæval teachers of melody; nor even melodies already extant, round which, as round a framework of pure music, their thoughts and images might crystallise themselves, certain thereby of becoming musical likewise. The best modern song writers, Burns and Moore, were inspired by their old national airs; and followed them, Moore at least, with a reverent fidelity, which has had its full reward. They wrote words to music; and not, as modern poets are wont, wrote the words first, and left others to set music to the words. They were right; and we are wrong. As long as song is to be the expression of pure emotion, so long it must take its key from music,—which is already pure emotion, untranslated into the grosser medium of thought and speech—often (as in the case of Mendelssohn's Songs without Words) not to be translated into it at all.

And so it may be that, in some simpler age, poets may go back, like the old Minnesingers, to the birds of the forest, and learn of them to sing.

And little do most of them know how much there is to learn; what variety of character, as well as variety of emotion, may be distinguished by the

practised ear in a "charm of birds" (to use the old
southern phrase), from the wild cry of the missel-
thrush, ringing from afar in the first bright days of
March, a passage of one or two bars repeated three
or four times, and then another and another, clear
and sweet, and yet defiant—for the great "storm-
cock" loves to sing when rain and wind is coming
on, and faces the elements as boldly as he faces
hawk and crow—down to the delicate warble of
the wren, who slips out of his hole in the brown
bank, where he has huddled through the frost with
wife and children, all folded in each other's arms
like human beings, for the sake of warmth,—
which, alas! does not always suffice; for many a
lump of wrens may be found, frozen and shrivelled,
after a severe winter. Yet even he, sitting at his
house-door in the low sunlight, says grace for all
mercies (as a little child once worded it) in a song
so rapid, so shrill, so loud, and yet so delicately
modulated, that you wonder at the amount of soul
within that tiny body; and then stops suddenly, as
a child who has said its lesson, or got to the end
of the sermon, gives a self-satisfied flirt of his tail,
and goes in again to sleep.

Character? I know not how much variety of
character there may be between birds of the same
species: but between species and species the variety
is endless, and is shown—as I fondly believe—in the
difference of their notes. Each has its own speech,
inarticulate, expressing not thought but hereditary
feeling; save a few birds who, like those little

71

dumb darlings, the spotted flycatchers, seem to have absolutely nothing to say, and accordingly have the wit to hold their tongues; and devote the whole of their small intellect to sitting on the iron rails, flitting off them a yard or two to catch a butterfly in air, and flitting back with it to their nest.

But to return, listen to birds in any sequestered woodland, on a bright forenoon in June. As you try to disentangle the medley of sounds, the first, perhaps, which will strike your ear will be the loud, harsh, monotonous, flippant song of the chaffinch; and the metallic clinking of two or three sorts of titmice. But above the tree-tops, rising, hovering, sinking, the woodlark is fluting, tender and low. Above the pastures outside the skylark sings—as he alone can sing; and close by, from the hollies rings out the blackbird's tenor—rollicking, audacious, humorous, all but articulate. From the tree above him rises the treble of the thrush, pure as the song of angels: more pure, perhaps, in tone, though neither so varied nor so rich, as the song of the nightingale. And there, in the next holly, is the nightingale himself: now croaking like a frog; now talking aside to his wife on the nest below; and now bursting out into that song, or cycle of songs, in which if any man finds sorrow, he himself surely finds none. All the morning he will sing; and again at evening, till the small hours, and the chill before the dawn: but if his voice sounds melancholy at night, heard all alone, or only mocked by the ambitious black-cap, it sounds in the bright morning that which it is, the fulness of joy and love. True, our own living poet tells us how

> In the topmost height of joy
> His passion clasps a secret grief.

Coleridge may have been too severe when he guessed that—

> Some night-wandering man, whose heart was pierced
> With the remembrance of a grievous wrong,
> Or slow distemper, or neglected love
> (And so, poor wretch, filled all things with himself,
> And made all gentle sounds tell back the tale
> Of his own sorrow)—he, and such as he,
> First named these sounds a melancholy strain,
> And many a poet echoes the conceit.

But that the old Greek poets were right, and had some grounds for the myth of Philomela, I do not dispute; though Sophocles, speaking of the nightingales of Colonos, certainly does not represent them as lamenting. The Elizabethan poets, however, when they talked of Philomel, "her breast against a thorn," were unaware that they and the Greeks were talking of two different birds; that our English Lusciola Luscinia is not Lusciola Philomela, one of the various birds called Bulbul in the East. The true Philomel hardly enters Venetia, hardly crosses the Swiss Alps, ventures not into the Rhine-land and Denmark, but penetrates (strangely enough) farther into South Sweden than our own Luscinia: ranging meanwhile over all Central Europe, Persia, and the East, even to Egypt. Whether his song be really sad, let those who have heard him say. But as for our own Luscinia, who winters not in Egypt and Arabia, but in Morocco and Algeria, the only note of his which can be mistaken for sorrow is rather one of too great joy; that cry, which is his highest feat of art; which he cannot utter when he first comes to our shores, but practises carefully, slowly, gradually, till he has it perfect by the beginning of June; that cry, long, repeated, loudening and sharpening in the intensity of rising passion, till it stops suddenly, exhausted at the point where pleasure, from very keenness, turns to pain.

How different in character from his song is that of the gallant little black-cap in the tree above him. A gentleman he is of a most ancient house, perhaps the oldest of European singing birds. How perfect must have been the special organisation which has spread, seemingly without need of altera-tion or improvement, from Norway to the Cape of Good Hope, from Japan to the Azores. How many ages must have passed since his forefathers first got their black caps. And how intense and fruitful must have been the original vitality which, after so many generations, can still fill that little body with so strong a soul, and make him sing as Milton's new-created birds sang to Milton's Eve in Milton's Paradise. Sweet he is, and various, rich, and strong, beyond all English warblers, save the nightingale: but his speciality is his force, his rush, his overflow, not so much of love as of happiness. The spirit carries him away. He riots up and down the gamut till he cannot stop himself; his notes tumble over each other; he chuckles, laughs, shrieks with delight, throws back his head, droops his tail, sets up his back, and sings with every fibre of his body: and yet he never forgets his good manners. He is never coarse, never harsh, for a single note. Always graceful, always sweet, he keeps perfect delicacy in his most utter carelessness.

And why should we overlook, common though he be, yon hedge-sparrow, who is singing so modestly, and yet so firmly and so true? Or cock-robin himself, who is here, as everywhere, honest, self-confident, and cheerful? Most people are not aware, one sometimes fancies, how fine a singer is cock-robin now in the spring-time, when his song is drowned by, or at least confounded with, a dozen other songs. We know him and love him best in winter, when he takes up (as he does sometimes in cold wet summer days) that sudden wistful warble, struggling to be happy, half in vain, which surely contradicts Coleridge's verse:

In Nature there is nothing melancholy.

But he who will listen carefully to the robin's breeding song on a bright day in May will agree, I think, that he is no mean musician; and that for force, variety and character of melody he is surpassed only by black-cap, thrush, and nightingale.

And what is that song, sudden, loud, sweet, yet faltering, as if half ashamed? Is it the willow wren or the garden warbler? The two birds, though very

75

remotely allied to each other, are so alike in voice, that it is often difficult to distinguish them, unless we attend carefully to the expression. For the garden warbler, beginning in high and loud notes, runs down in cadence, lower and softer, till joy seems conquered by very weariness; while the willow wren, with a sudden outbreak of cheerfulness, though not quite sure (it is impossible to describe bird-songs without attributing to the birds human passions and frailties) that he is not doing a silly thing, struggles on to the end of his story with a hesitating hilarity, in feeble imitation of the black-cap's bacchanalian dactyls.

And now, again—is it true that

In Nature there is nothing melancholy?

Mark that slender, graceful, yellow warbler, running along the high oak boughs like a perturbed spirit, seeking restlessly, anxiously, something which he seems never to find; and uttering every now and then a long anxious cry, four or five times repeated, which would be a squeal were it not so sweet. Suddenly he flits away, and flutters round the pendent tips of the beech-sprays like a great yellow butterfly, picking the insects from the leaves; then flits back to a bare bough, and sings, with heaving breast and quivering wings, a short, shrill, feeble, tremulous song; and then returns to his old sadness, wandering and complaining all day long. Is there no melancholy in that cry? It sounds sad: why should it not be meant to be sad? We recognise joyful notes, angry notes, fearful notes. They are very similar (strangely enough) in all birds. They are very similar (more strangely still) to the cries of human beings, especially children, when influenced by the same passions. And when we hear a note which to us expresses sadness, why should not the bird be sad? Yon wood wren has had enough to make him sad, if only he recollects it; and if he can recollect his road from Morocco hither, he maybe recollects likewise what happened on the road—the long weary journey up the Portuguese coast, and through the gap between the Pyrenees and the Jaysquivel, and up the Landes of Bordeaux, and across Brittany, flitting by night, and hiding and feeding as he could by day; and how his mates flew against the lighthouses, and were killed by hundreds; and how he essayed the British Channel, and was blown back, shrivelled up by bitter blasts; and how he felt, nevertheless, that "that wan water he must cross," he knew not why: but something told him that his mother had done it before him, and he was flesh of her flesh, life of her life, and had inherited her "instinct" —as we call hereditary memory, in order to avoid the trouble of finding out what it is, and how it comes. A duty was laid on him to go back to the place where he was bred; and he must do it: and now it is done; and he is weary, and sad, and lonely; and, for aught we know, thinking already that when the leaves begin to turn yellow, he must go back again, over the Channel, over the Landes,

over the Pyrenees, to Morocco once more. Why
should he not be sad? He is a very delicate bird,
as both his shape and his note testify. He can
hardly keep up his race here in England; and is
accordingly very uncommon, while his two cousins,
the willow wren and the chiff-chaff, who, like him,
build for some mysterious reason domed nests upon
the ground, are stout, and busy, and numerous,
and thriving everywhere. And what he has gone
through may be too much for the poor wood wren's
nerves; and he gives way; while willow wren,
black-cap, nightingale, who have gone by the same
road and suffered the same dangers, have stoutness
of heart enough to throw off the past, and give
themselves up to present pleasure. Why not?—
who knows? There is labour, danger, bereavement, death in nature; and why should not some,
at least, of the so-called dumb things know it, and
grieve at it as well as we?

Why not?—Unless we yield to the assumption
(for it is nothing more) that these birds act by
some unknown thing called instinct, as it might be
called x or y; and are, in fact, just like the singing
birds which spring out of snuff-boxes, only so much
better made, that they can eat, grow, and propagate
their species. The imputation of acting by instinct
cuts both ways. We, too, are creatures of instinct.
We breathe and eat by instinct: but we talk and
build houses by reason. And so may the birds. It
is more philosophical, surely, to attribute actions
in them to the same causes to which we attribute

them (from experience) in ourselves. " But if so,"
some will say, " birds must have souls." We must
define what our own souls are, before we can define
what kind of soul or no-soul a bird may or may
not have. The truth is, that we want to set up
some " dignity of human nature "; some innate
superiority to the animals, on which we may
pride ourselves as our own possession, and not
return thanks with fear and trembling for it, as
the special gift of Almighty God. So we have
given the poor animals over to the mechanical
philosophy, and allowed them to be considered as
only mere cunningly devised pieces of watch-work,
if philosophy would only spare us, and our fine
human souls, of which we are so proud, though
they are doing all the wrong and folly they can
from one week's end to the other. And now our
self-conceit has brought its own Nemesis. The
mechanical philosophy is turning on us, and saying,
" The bird's ' nature ' and your ' human nature '
differ only in degree, but not in kind. If they are
machines, so are you. They have no souls, you
confess. You have none either."

But there are those who neither yield to the
mechanical philosophy nor desire to stifle it. While
it is honest and industrious, as it is now, it can do
nought but good, because it can do nought but
discover facts. It will only help to divide the light
from the darkness, truth from dreams, health from
disease. Let it claim for itself all that it can prove
to be of the flesh, fleshly. That which is spiritual

will stand out more clearly as of the Spirit. Let
it thrust scalpel and microscope into the most sacred
penetralia of brain and nerve. It will only find
everywhere beneath brain and beneath nerve that
substance and form which is not matter nor phenomenon, but the Divine cause thereof; and while
it helps, with ruthless but wholesome severity, to
purge our minds from idols of the cave and idols
of the fane, it will leave untouched, more clearly
defined, and therefore more sacred and important
than ever—

> Those first affections,
> Those shadowy recollections,
> Which, be they what they may,
> Are yet the fountain light of all our day,
> Are yet the master light of all our seeing;
> Uphold us, cherish, and have power to make
> Our noisy years seem moments in the being
> Of the eternal silence; truths that wake
> To perish never;
> Which neither listlessness, nor mad endeavour,
> Nor man nor boy,
> Nor all that is at enmity with joy,
> Can utterly abolish or destroy.

> .   .   .   .   .   .

> Then sing, ye birds, sing out with joyous sound,

as the poet-philosopher bids you. Victorious analysis
will neither abolish you, nor the miraculous and
unfathomable in you and in your song, which has
stirred the hearts of poets since first man was man.
And if any one shall hint to us that we and the birds
may have sprung originally from the same type;
that the difference between our intellect and theirs

is one of degree, and not of kind, we may believe or doubt: but in either case we shall not be greatly moved. " So much the better for the birds," we will say, " and none the worse for us. You raise the birds towards us: but you do not lower us towards them. What we are, we are by the grace of God. Our own powers and the burden of them we know full well. It does not lessen their dignity or their beauty in our eyes to hear that the birds of the air partake, even a little, of the same gifts of God as we. Of old said St. Guthlac in Crowland, as the swallows sat upon his knee, " He who leads his life according to the will of God, to him the wild deer and the wild birds draw more near "; and this new theory of yours may prove St. Guthlac right. St. Francis too, he called the birds his brothers. Whether he was correct, either theologically or zoologically, he was plainly free from that fear of being mistaken for an ape which haunts so many in these modern times. Perfectly sure that he himself was a spiritual being, he thought it at least possible that birds might be spiritual beings likewise, incarnate like himself in mortal flesh; and saw no degradation to the dignity of human nature in claiming kindred lovingly with creatures so beautiful, so wonderful, who (as he fancied in his old-fashioned way) praised God in the forest, even as angels did in heaven. In a word, the saint, though he was an ascetic, and certainly no man of science, was yet a poet, and somewhat of a philosopher; and would have possibly—so do extremes meet—

have hailed as orthodox, while we hail as truly
scientific, Wordsworth's great saying—

> Therefore am I still
> A lover of the meadows and the woods
> And mountains; and of all that we behold
> From this green earth; of all the mighty world
> Of eye and ear—both what they half create,
> And what perceive; well pleased to recognise
> In Nature and the language of the sense,
> The anchor of my purest thoughts, the nurse,
> The guide, the guardian of my heart, and soul
> Of all my moral being.

OLD AGE

By Ralph Waldo Emerson

On the anniversary of the Phi Beta Kappa Society at Cambridge, in 1861, the venerable President Quincy, senior member of the Society, as well as senior alumnus of the University, was received at the dinner with peculiar demonstrations of respect. He replied to these compliments in a speech; and, gracefully claiming the privileges of a literary society, entered at some length into an Apology for Old Age; and, aiding himself by notes in his hand, made a sort of running commentary on Cicero's chapter *De Senectute*. The character of the speaker, the transparent good faith of his praise and blame, and the *naïveté* of his eager preference of Cicero's opinions to King David's, gave unusual interest to the College festival. It was a discourse full of dignity, honouring him who spoke and those who heard.

The speech led me to look over at home—an easy task—Cicero's famous essay, charming by its uniform rhetorical merit; heroic with Stoical precepts; with a Roman eye to the claims of the State; happiest, perhaps, in his praise of life on the farm; and rising at the conclusion to a lofty strain. But he does not exhaust the subject; rather invites the attempt to add traits to the picture from our broader modern life.

Cicero makes no reference to the illusions which cling to the element of time, and in which Nature delights. Wellington, in speaking of military men, said, " What masks are these uniforms to hide cowards! " I have often detected the like deception in the cloth shoe, wadded pelisse, wig, spectacles, and padded chair of Age. Nature lends herself to these illusions, and adds dim sight, deafness, cracked voice, snowy hair, short memory, and sleep. These also are masks, and all is not Age that wears them. Whilst we yet call ourselves young, and our mates are yet youths, with even boyish remains, one good fellow in the set prematurely sports a grey or a bald head, which does not impose on us who know how innocent of sanctity or of Platonism he is, but does deceive his juniors and the public, who presently distinguish him with a most amusing respect; and this lets us into the secret, that the venerable forms that so awed our childhood were just such impostors. Nature is full of freaks, and now puts an old head on young shoulders, and then a young heart beating under fourscore winters.

For if the essence of age is not present, these signs, whether of Art or Nature, are counterfeit and ridiculous; and the essence of age is intellect. Wherever that appears, we call it old. If we look into the eyes of the youngest person, we sometimes discover that here is one who knows already what you would go about with much pains to teach him; there is that in him which is the ancestor of all around him: which fact the Indian Vedas express when they say, " He that can discriminate is the father of his father." And in our old British legends of Arthur and the Round Table, his friend and counsellor, Merlin the Wise, is a babe found exposed in a basket by the river-side; and, though an infant of only a few days, speaks articulately to those who discover him, tells his name and history, and presently foretells the fate of the bystanders. Wherever there is power, there is age. Don't be deceived by dimples and curls. I tell you that babe is a thousand years old.

Time is, indeed, the theatre and seat of illusion: nothing is so ductile and elastic. The mind stretches an hour to a century, and dwarfs an age to an hour. Saadi found in a mosque at Damascus an old Persian of a hundred and fifty years, who was dying, and was saying to himself, " I said, coming into the world by birth, ' I will enjoy myself for a few moments.' Alas; at the variegated table of life I partook of a few mouthfuls, and the Fates said, ' *Enough !* ' " That which does not decay is so central and controlling in us, that, as long as one is alone by himself, he is not sensible of the inroads of time, which always begin at the surface-edges. If, on a winter day, you should stand within a bell-glass, the face and colour of the afternoon clouds would not indicate whether it were June or January; and if we did not find the reflection of ourselves in the eyes of the young people, we could not know that the century-clock had struck seventy instead of twenty How many men habitually believe that each chance passenger with whom they converse is of their own age, and presently find it was his father, and not his brother, whom they knew!

But not to press too hard on these deceits and illusions of Nature, which are inseparable from our condition, and looking at age under an aspect more conformed to the common sense, if the question be the felicity of age, I fear the first popular judgments will be unfavourable. From the point of sensuous experience, seen from the streets and markets and the haunts of pleasure and gain, the estimate of age is low, melancholy, and sceptical. Frankly face the facts, and see the result. Tobacco, coffee, alcohol, hashish, prussic acid, strychnine, are weak dilutions: the surest poison is time. This cup, which Nature puts to our lips, has a wonderful virtue, surpassing that of any other draught. It opens the senses, adds power, fills us with exalted dreams, which we call hope, love, ambition, science: especially, it creates a craving for larger draughts of itself. But they who take the larger draughts are drunk with it, lose their stature, strength, beauty, and senses, and end in folly and delirium. We postpone our literary work until we have more ripeness and skill to write, and we one day discover that our literary talent was a youthful effervescence which we have now lost. We had a judge in

Massachusetts who at sixty proposed to resign, alleging that he perceived a certain decay in his faculties; he was dissuaded by his friends, on account of the public convenience at that time. At seventy it was hinted to him that it was time to retire; but he now replied, that he thought his judgment as robust, and all his faculties as good as ever they were. But besides the self-deception, the strong and hasty labourers of the street do not work well with the chronic valetudinarian. Youth is everywhere in place. Age, like woman, requires fit surroundings. Age is comely in coaches, in churches, in chairs of state, and ceremony, in council chambers, in courts of justice, and historical societies. Age is becoming in the country. But in the rush and uproar of Broadway, if you look into the faces of the passengers, there is dejection or indignation in the seniors, a certain concealed sense of injury, and the lip made up with a heroic determination not to mind it. Few envy the consideration enjoyed by the oldest inhabitant. We do not count a man's years until he has nothing else to count. The vast inconvenience of animal immortality was told in the fable of Tithonus. In short, the creed of the street is, Old Age is not disgraceful, but immensely disadvantageous. Life is well enough, but we shall all be glad to get out of it, and they will all be glad to have us.

This is odious on the face of it. Universal convictions are not to be shaken by the whimseys of overfed butchers and firemen, or by the sentimental

fears of girls who would keep the infantile bloom
on their cheeks. We know the value of experience.
Life and art are cumulative; and he who has
accomplished something in any department alone
deserves to be heard on that subject. A man of
great employments and excellent performance used
to assure me that he did not think a man worth
anything until he was sixty; although this smacks
a little of the resolution of a certain " Young Men's
Republican Club," that all men should be held
eligible who were under seventy. But in all governments, the councils of power were held by the old;
and patricians or *patres*, senate or *senes*, *seigneurs*
or seniors, *gerousia*, the senate of Sparta, the pres-
bytery of the Church, and the like, all signify
simply old men.

The cynical creed or lampoon of the market is
refuted by the universal prayer for long life, which
is the verdict of Nature, and justified by all history.
We have, it is true, examples of an accelerated pace
by which young men achieved grand works; as
in the Macedonian Alexander, in Raffaelle, Shakespeare, Pascal, Burns, and Byron; but these are
rare exceptions. Nature, in the main, vindicates
her law. Skill to do comes of doing; knowledge
comes by eyes always open, and working hands;
and there is no knowledge that is not power.
Béranger said, " Almost all the good workmen live
long." And if the life be true and noble, we have
quite another sort of seniors than the frowzy,
timorous, peevish dotards who are falsely old—

namely, the men who fear no city, but by whom cities stand; who appearing in any street, the people empty their houses to gaze at and obey them: as at " My Cid, with the fleecy beard," in Toledo; or Bruce, as Barbour reports him; as blind old Dandolo, elected Doge at eighty-four years, storming Constantinople at ninety-four, and after the revolt again victorious, and elected at the age of ninety-six to the throne of the Eastern empire, which he declined, and died Doge at ninety-seven. We still feel the force of Socrates, " whom well-advised the oracle pronounced wisest of men "; of Archimedes, holding Syracuse against the Romans by his wit, and himself better than all their nation; of Michael Angelo, wearing the four crowns of architecture, sculpture, painting, and poetry; of Galileo, of whose blindness Castelli said: " The noblest eye is darkened that Nature ever made—an eye that hath seen more than all that went before him, and hath opened the eyes of all that shall come after him "; of Newton, who made an important discovery for every one of his eighty-five years; of Bacon, who " took all knowledge to be his province "; of Fontenelle, " that precious porcelain vase laid up in the centre of France to be guarded with the utmost care for a hundred years "; of Franklin, Jefferson, and Adams, the wise and heroic statesmen; of Washington, the perfect citizen; of Wellington, the perfect soldier; of Goethe, the all-knowing poet; of Humboldt, the encyclopædia of science.

Under the general assertion of the well-being of age, we can easily count particular benefits of that condition. It has weathered the perilous capes and shoals in the sea whereon we sail, and the chief evil of life is taken away in removing the grounds of fear. The insurance of a ship expires as she enters the harbour at home. It were strange, if a man should turn his sixtieth year without a feeling of immense relief from the number of dangers he has escaped. When the old wife says, " Take care of that tumour in your shoulder, perhaps it is cancerous,"—he replies, " I am yielding to a surer decomposition." The humorous thief who drank a pot of beer at the gallows blew off the froth because he had heard it was unhealthy; but it will not add a pang to the prisoner marched out to be shot to assure him that the pain in his knee threatens mortification. When the pleuro-pneumonia of the cows raged, the butcher said, that though the acute degree was novel, there never was a time when this disease did not occur among cattle. All men carry seeds of all distempers through life latent, and we die without developing them; such is the affirmative force of the constitution; but if you are enfeebled by any cause, some of these sleeping seeds start and open. Meantime, at every stage we lose a foe. At fifty years, 'tis said, afflicted citizens lose their sick-headaches. I hope this *hegira* is not as movable a feast as that one I annually look for, when the horticulturists assure me that the rose-bugs in our garden disappear on the tenth of

July; they stay a fortnight later in mine. But be it as it may with the sick-headache, 'tis certain that graver headaches and heart-aches are lulled once for all, as we come up with certain goals of time. The passions have answered their purpose; that slight but dread overweight, with which, in each instance, Nature secures the execution of her aim, drops off. To keep man in the planet, she impresses the terror of death. To perfect the commissariat, she implants in each a certain rapacity to get the supply, and a little over-supply, of his wants. To insure the existence of the race, she reinforces the sexual instinct, at the risk of disorder, grief, and pain. To secure strength, she plants cruel hunger and thirst, which so easily overdo their office, and invite disease. But these temporary stays and shifts, for the protection of the young animal, are shed as fast as they can be replaced by nobler resources. We live in youth amidst this rabble of passions, quite too tender, quite too hungry and irritable. Later, the interiors of mind and heart open, and supply grander motives. We learn the fatal compensations that wait on every act. Then — one after another — this riotous time-destroying crew disappear.

I count it another capital advantage of age, this, that a success more or less signifies nothing. Little by little, it has amassed such a fund of merit, that it can very well afford to go on its credit when it will. When I chanced to meet the poet Wordsworth, then sixty-three years old, he told me " that he had just had a fall and lost a tooth, and, when his companions were much concerned for the mischance, he had replied, that he was glad it had not happened forty years before." Well, Nature takes care that we shall not lose our organs forty years too soon. A lawyer argued a cause yesterday in the Supreme Court, and I was struck with a certain air of levity and defiance which vastly became him. Thirty years ago it was a serious concern to him whether his pleading was good and effective. Now it is of importance to his client, but of none to himself. It has been long already fixed what he can do and cannot do, and his reputation does not gain or suffer from one or a dozen new performances. If he should, on a new occasion, rise quite beyond his mark, and achieve somewhat great and extraordinary, that, of course, would instantly tell; but he may go below his mark with impunity, and people will say, "Oh, he had headache," or, "He lost his sleep for two nights." What a lust of appearance, what a load of anxieties that once degraded him, he is thus rid of! Every one is sensible of this cumulative advantage in living. All the good days behind him are sponsors, who speak for him when he is silent, pay for him when he has no money, introduce him where he has no letters, and work for him when he sleeps.

A third felicity of age is, that it has found expression. The youth suffers not only from ungratified desires, but from powers untried, and from a picture in his mind of a career which has, as yet, no outward reality. He is tormented with the want of correspondence between things and thoughts. Michael Angelo's head is full of masculine and gigantic figures, as gods walking, which make him savage until his furious chisel can render them into marble; and of architectural dreams, until a hundred stone-masons can lay them in courses of travertine. There is the like tempest in every good head in which some great benefit for the world is planted. The throes continue until the child is born. Every faculty new to each man thus goads him and drives him out into doleful deserts, until it finds proper vent. All the functions of human duty irritate and lash him forward, bemoaning and chiding, until they are performed. He wants friends, employment, knowledge, power, house and land, wife and children, honour and fame; he has religious wants, æsthetic wants, domestic, civil, humane wants. One by one, day after day, he learns to coin his wishes into facts. He has his calling, homestead, social connection, and personal power, and thus, at the end of fifty years, his soul is appeased by seeing some sort of correspondence between his wish and his possession. This makes the value of age, the satisfaction it slowly offers to every craving. He is serene who does not feel himself pinched and wronged, but whose condition, in particular and in general, allows the utterance of his mind. In old persons, when thus fully expressed, we often observe a fair, plump, perennial, waxen complexion, which indicates that all the ferment of earlier days has subsided into serenity of thought and behaviour.

The compensations of Nature play in age as in youth. In a world so charged and sparkling with power, a man does not live long and actively without costly additions of experience, which, though not spoken, are recorded in his mind. What to the youth is only a guess or a hope, is in the veteran a digested statute. He beholds the feats of the juniors with complacency, but as one who, having long ago known these games, has refined them into results and morals. The Indian Red Jacket, when the young braves were boasting their deeds, said, " But the sixties have all the twenties and forties in them."

For a fourth benefit, age sets its house in order, and finishes its works, which to every artist is a supreme pleasure. Youth has an excess of sensibility, before which every object glitters and attracts. We leave one pursuit for another, and the young man's year is a heap of beginnings. At the end of a twelvemonth, he had nothing to show for it,—not one completed work. But the time is not lost. Our instincts drove us to hive innumerable experiences, that are yet of no visible value, and which we may keep for twice seven years before they shall be wanted. The best things are of secular growth. The instinct of classifying marks the wise and healthy mind. Linnæus projects his system, and lays out his twenty-four classes of plants, before yet he has found in Nature a single plant

94

to justify certain of his classes. His seventh class has not one. In process of time, he finds with delight the little white *Trientalis*, the only plant with seven petals and sometimes seven stamens, which constitutes a seventh class in conformity with his system. The conchologist builds his cabinet whilst as yet he has few shells. He labels shelves for classes, cells for species: all but a few are empty. But every year fills some blanks, and with accelerating speed as he becomes knowing and known. An old scholar finds keen delight in verifying the impressive anecdotes and citations he has met with in miscellaneous reading and hearing, in all the years of youth. We carry in memory important anecdotes, and have lost all clue to the author from whom we had them. We have a heroic speech from Rome or Greece, but cannot fix it on the man who said it. We have an admirable line worthy of Horace, ever and anon resounding in our mind's ear, but have searched all probable and improbable books for it in vain. We consult the reading men; but, strangely enough, they who know everything know not this. But especially we have a certain insulated thought, which haunts us, but remains insulated and barren. Well, there is nothing for all this but patience and time. Time, yes, that is the finder, the unweariable explorer, not subject to casualties, omniscient at last. The day comes when the hidden author of our story is found; when the brave speech returns straight to the hero who said it; when the admirable verse finds the

poet to whom it belongs; and best of all, when the
lonely thought, which seemed so wise, yet half-
wise, half-thought, because it cast no light abroad,
is suddenly matched in our mind by its twin, by its
sequence, or next related analogy, which gives it
instantly radiating power, and justifies the super-
stitious instinct with which we have hoarded it.
We remember our old Greek professor at Cambridge, and ancient bachelor, amid his folios,
possessed by this hope of completing a task, with
nothing to break his leisure after the three hours
of his daily classes, yet ever restlessly stroking his
leg, and assuring himself " he should retire from
the University and read the authors." In Goethe's
romance, Makaria, the central figure for wisdom
and influence, pleases herself with withdrawing
into solitude to astronomy and epistolary correspondence. Goethe himself carried this completion
of studies to the highest point. Many of his works
hung on the easel from youth to age, and received
a stroke in every month or year. A literary astro-
loger, he never applied himself to any task but at
the happy moment when all the stars consented.
Bentley thought himself likely to live till fourscore,
—long enough to read everything that was worth
reading,—" *Et tunc magna mei sub terris ibit
imago.*" Much wider is spread the pleasure which
old men take in completing their secular affairs,
the inventor his inventions, the agriculturist his
experiments, and all old men in finishing their
houses, rounding their estates, clearing their titles,

reducing tangled interests to order, reconciling enmities, and leaving all in the best posture for the future. It must be believed that there is a proportion between the designs of a man and the length of his life: there is a calendar of his years, so of his performances.

America is the country of young men, and too full of work hitherto for leisure and tranquillity; yet we have had robust centenarians, and examples of dignity and wisdom. I have lately found in an old note-book a record of a visit to ex-President John Adams, in 1825, soon after the election of his son to the Presidency. It is but a sketch, and nothing important passed in the conversation; but it reports a moment in the life of a heroic person, who, in extreme old age, appeared still erect and worthy of his fame.

—— *Feb.* 1825. —— To-day, at Quincy, with my brother by invitation of Mr. Adams's family. The old President sat in a large stuffed arm-chair, dressed in a blue coat, black small-clothes, white stockings; a cotton cap covered his bald head. We made our compliment, told him he must let us join our congratulations to those of the nation on the happiness of his house. He thanked us, and said: "I am rejoiced, because the nation is happy. The time of gratulation and congratulations is nearly over with me: I am astonished that I have lived to see and know of this event. I have lived now nearly a century [he was ninety in the following

October]; a long, harassed, and distracted life."—
I said, " The world thinks a good deal of joy has
been mixed with it."—" The world does not
know," he replied, " how much toil, anxiety, and
sorrow I have suffered."—I asked if Mr. Adams's
letter of acceptance had been read to him.—
" Yes," he said, and added, " My son has more
political prudence than any man that I know who
has existed in my time; he never was put off his
guard: and I hope he will continue such; but
what effect age may work in diminishing the
power of his mind, I do not know; it has been
very much on the stretch, ever since he was born.
He has always been laborious, child and man, from
infancy."—When Mr. J. Q. Adams's age was
mentioned, he said, " He is now fifty-eight, or will
be in July "; and remarked that " all the Presidents
were of the same age: General Washington was
about fifty-eight, and I was about fifty-eight, and
Mr. Jefferson, and Mr. Madison, and Mr. Monroe."
—We inquired when he expected to see Mr.
Adams.—He said: " Never: Mr. Adams will not
come to Quincy, but to my funeral. It would be
a great satisfaction to me to see him, but I don't
wish him to come on my account."—He spoke of
Mr. Lechmere, whom he " well remembered to
have seen come down daily, at a great age, to walk
in the old town-house,"—adding, " and I wish I
could walk as well as he did. He was Collector
of the Customs for many years under the Royal
Government."—E. said: " I suppose, sir, you

would not have taken his place, even to walk as well as he."—" No," he replied, " that was not what I wanted." He talked of Whitefield, and " remembered when he was a freshman in college, to have come into town to the *Old South* church, I think, to hear him, but could not get into the house;—I, however, saw him," he said, " through a window, and distinctly heard all. He had a voice such as I never heard before or since. He cast it out so that you might hear it at the meeting-house —pointing towards the Quincy meeting-house— and he had the grace of a dancing-master, of an actor of plays. His voice and manner helped him more than his sermons. I went with Jonathan Sewall."—" And you were pleased with him, sir? " —" Pleased! I was delighted beyond measure." —We asked, if at Whitefield's return the same popularity continued.—" Not the same fury," he said, " not the same wild enthusiasm as before, but a greater esteem, as he became more known. He did not terrify, but was admired."

We spent about an hour in his room. He speaks very distinctly for so old a man, enters bravely into long sentences, which are interrupted by want of breath, but carries them invariably to a conclusion, without correcting a word.

He spoke of the new novels of Cooper, and *Peep at the Pilgrims,* and *Saratoga,* with praise, and named with accuracy the characters in them. He likes to have a person always reading to him, or company talking in his room, and is better the next day after having visitors in his chamber from morning to night.

He received a premature report of his son's election, on Sunday afternoon, without any excitement, and told the reporter he had been hoaxed, for it was not yet time for any news to arrive. The informer, something damped in his heart, insisted on repairing to the meeting-house, and proclaimed it aloud to the congregation, who were so overjoyed that they rose in their seats and cheered thrice. The Rev. Mr. Whitney dismissed them immediately.

When life has been well spent, age is a loss of what it can well spare,—muscular strength, organic instincts, gross bulk, and works that belong to these. But the central wisdom, which was old in infancy, is young in fourscore years, and, dropping off obstructions, leaves in happy subjects the mind purified and wise. I have heard that whoever loves is in no condition old. I have heard, that, whenever the name of man is spoken, the doctrine of immortality is announced: it cleaves to his constitution. The mode of it baffles our wit, and no whisper comes to us from the other side. But the inference from the working of intellect, hiving knowledge, hiving skill,—at the end of life just ready to be born,—affirms the inspirations of affection and of the moral sentiment.

THOREAU

By James Russell Lowell

What contemporary, if he was in the fighting period of his life (since Nature sets limits about her conscription for spiritual fields, as the state does in physical warfare), will ever forget what was somewhat vaguely called the "Transcendental Movement" of thirty years ago? Apparently set astirring by Carlyle's essays on the "Signs of the Times," and on "History," the final and more immediate impulse seemed to be given by *Sartor Resartus*. At least the republication in Boston of that wonderful Abraham à Sancta Clara sermon on Lear's text of the miserable forked radish gave the signal for a sudden mental and moral mutiny. *Ecce nunc tempus acceptabile!* was shouted on all hands with every variety of emphasis, and by voices of every conceivable pitch, representing the three sexes of men, women, and Lady Mary Wortley Montagues. The nameless eagle of the tree Ygdrasil was about to sit at last, and wild-eyed enthusiasts rushed from all sides, each eager to thrust under the mystic bird that chalk egg from which the new and fairer Creation was to be hatched in due time. *Redeunt Saturnia regna*—so far was certain, though in

what shape, or by what methods, was still a matter
of debate. Every possible form of intellectual and
physical dyspepsia brought forth its gospel. Bran
had its prophets, and the presartorial simplicity of
Adam its martyrs, tailored impromptu from the
tar-pot by incensed neighbours, and sent forth to
illustrate the " feathered Mercury," as defined by
Webster and Worcester. Plainness of speech was
carried to a pitch that would have taken away the
breath of George Fox; and even swearing had its
evangelists, who answered a simple inquiry after
their health with an elaborate ingenuity of im-
precation that might have been honourably mentioned by Marlborough in general orders. Everybody had a mission (with a capital M) to attend
to everybody-else's business. No brain but had its
private maggot, which must have found pitiably
short commons sometimes. Not a few impecunious
zealots abjured the use of money (unless earned by
other people), professing to live on the internal
revenues of the spirit. Some had an assurance of
instant millennium so soon as hooks and eyes
should be substituted for buttons. Communities
were established where everything was to be common
but common-sense. Men renounced their old
gods, and hesitated only whether to bestow their
furloughed allegiance on Thor or Buddha. Con-
ventions were held for every hitherto inconceivable
purpose. The belated gift of tongues, as among
the Fifth Monarchy men, spread like a contagion,
rendering its victims incomprehensible to all

Christian men; whether equally so to the most distant possible heathen or not was unexperimented, though many would have subscribed liberally that a fair trial might be made. It was the pentecost of Shinar. The day of utterances reproduced the day of rebuses and anagrams, and there was nothing so simple that uncial letters and the style of Diphilus the Labyrinth could not turn into a riddle. Many foreign revolutionists out of work added to the general misunderstanding their contribution of broken English in every most ingenious form of fracture. All stood ready at a moment's notice to reform everything but themselves. The general motto was:

> And we'll *talk* with them, too,
> And take upon 's the mystery of things
> As if we were God's spies.

Nature is always kind enough to give even her clouds a humorous lining. We have barely hinted at the comic side of the affair, for the material was endless. This was the whistle and trailing fuse of the shell, but there was a very solid and serious kernel, full of the most deadly explosiveness. Thoughtful men divined it, but the generality suspected nothing. The word " transcendental " then was the maid-of-all-work for those who could not think, as " Pre-Raphaelite " has been more recently for people of the same limited house-keeping. The truth is, that there was a much nearer metaphysical relation and a much more distant æsthetic and literary relation between

Carlyle and the Apostles of the Newness, as they were called in New England, than has commonly been supposed. Both represented the reaction and revolt against *Philisterei*, a renewal of the old battle begun in modern times by Erasmus and Reuchlin, and continued by Lessing, Goethe, and, in a far narrower sense, by Heine in Germany, and of which Fielding, Sterne, and Wordsworth in different ways have been the leaders in England. It was simply a struggle for fresh air, in which, if the windows could not be opened, there was danger that panes would be broken, though painted with images of saints and martyrs. Light coloured by these reverend effigies was none the more respirable for being picturesque. There is only one thing better than tradition, and that is the original and eternal life out of which all tradition takes its rise. It was this life which the reformers demanded, with more or less clearness of consciousness and expression, life in politics, life in literature, life in religion. Of what use to import a gospel from Judæa, if we leave behind the soul that made it possible, the God who keeps it for ever real and present? Surely Abana and Pharpar *are* better than Jordan, if a living faith be mixed with those waters and none with these.

Scotch Presbyterianism as a motive of spiritual progress was dead; New England Puritanism was in like manner dead; in other words, Protestantism had made its fortune and no longer protested; but till Carlyle spoke out in the Old World and

Emerson in the New, no one had dared to proclaim, *Le roi est mort: vive le roi!* The meaning of which proclamation was essentially this: the vital spirit has long since departed out of this form once so kingly, and the great seal has been in commission long enough; but meanwhile the soul of man, from which all power emanates and to which it reverts, still survives in undiminished royalty; God still survives, little as you gentlemen of the Commission seem to be aware of it—nay, may possibly outlive the whole of you, incredible as it may appear. The truth is, that both Scotch Presbyterianism and New England Puritanism made their new avatar in Carlyle and Emerson, the heralds of their formal decease, and the tendency of the one toward Authority and of the other toward Independency might have been prophesied by whoever had studied history. The necessity was not so much in the men as in the principles they represented and the traditions which overruled them. The Puritanism of the past found its unwilling poet in Hawthorne, the rarest creative imagination of the century, the rarest in some ideal respects since Shakespeare; but the Puritanism that cannot die, the Puritanism that made New England what it is, and is destined to make America what it should be, found its voice in Emerson. Though holding himself aloof from all active partnership in movements of reform, he has been the sleeping partner who has supplied a great part of their capital.

The artistic range of Emerson is narrow, as

every well-read critic must feel at once; and so is that of Æschylus, so is that of Dante, so is that of Montaigne, so is that of Schiller, so is that of nearly every one except Shakespeare; but there is a gauge of height no less than of breadth, of individuality as well as of comprehensiveness, and, above all, there is the standard of genetic power, the test of the masculine as distinguished from the receptive minds. There are staminate plants in literature, that make no fine show of fruit, but without whose pollen, quintessence of fructifying gold, the garden had been barren. Emerson's mind is emphatically one of these, and there is no man to whom our æsthetic culture owes so much. The Puritan revolt had made us ecclesiastically, and the Revolution politically independent, but we were still socially and intellectually moored to English thought, till Emerson cut the cable and gave us a chance at the dangers and the glories of blue water. No man young enough to have felt it can forget, or cease to be grateful for, the mental and moral *nudge* which he received from the writings of his high-minded and brave-spirited countryman. That we agree with him, or that he always agrees with himself, is aside from the question; but that he arouses in us something that we are the better for having awakened, whether that something be of opposition or assent, that he speaks always to what is highest and least selfish in us, few Americans of the generation younger than his own would be disposed to deny. His oration before the Phi Beta Kappa

Society at Cambridge, some thirty years ago, was an event without any former parallel in our literary annals, a scene to be always treasured in the memory for its picturesqueness and its inspiration. What crowded and breathless aisles, what windows clustering with eager heads, what enthusiasm of approval, what grim silence of foregone dissent! It was our Yankee version of a lecture by Abelard, our Harvard parallel to the last public appearances of Schelling.

We said that the Transcendental Movement was the Protestant spirit of Puritanism seeking a new outlet and an escape from forms and creeds which compressed rather than expressed it. In its motives, its preaching, and its results, it differed radically from the doctrine of Carlyle. The Scotchman, with all his genius, and his humour gigantesque as that of Rabelais, has grown shriller and shriller with years, degenerating sometimes into a common scold, and emptying very unsavoury vials of wrath on the head of the sturdy British Socrates of worldly common-sense. The teaching of Emerson tended much more exclusively to self-culture and the independent development of the individual man. It seemed to many almost Pythagorean in its voluntary seclusion from commonwealth affairs. Both Carlyle and Emerson were disciples of Goethe, but Emerson in a far truer sense; and while the one, from his bias toward the eccentric, has degenerated more and more into mannerism, the other has clarified steadily toward perfection of style—

exquisite fineness of material, unobtrusive lowness of tone and simplicity of fashion, the most high-bred garb of expression. Whatever may be said of his thought, nothing can be finer than the delicious limpidness of his phrase. If it was ever questionable whether democracy could develop a gentleman, the problem has been affirmatively solved at last. Carlyle, in his cynicism and his admiration of force in and for itself, has become at last positively inhuman; Emerson, reverencing strength, seeking the highest outcome of the individual, has found that society and politics are also main elements in the attainment of the desired end, and has drawn steadily manward and world-ward. The two men represent respectively those grand personifications in the drama of Æschylus, Βία and Κράτος.

Among the pistillate plants kindled to fruitage by the Emersonian pollen, Thoreau is thus far the most remarkable; and it is something eminently fitting that his posthumous works should be offered us by Emerson, for they are strawberries from his own garden. A singular mixture of varieties, indeed, there is;—alpine, some of them, with the flavour of real mountain air; others wood, tasting of sunny roadside banks or shy openings in the forest; and not a few seedlings swollen hugely by culture, but lacking the fine natural aroma of the more modest kinds. Strange books these are of his, and interesting in many ways—instructive chiefly as showing how considerable a crop may be raised on a comparatively narrow close of mind, and how much a man may make of his life if he will assiduously follow it, though perhaps never truly finding it at last.

We have just been renewing our recollection of Mr Thoreau's writings, and have read through his six volumes in the order of their production. We shall try to give an adequate report of their impression upon us both as critic and as mere reader. He seems to us to have been a man with so high a conceit of himself that he accepted without questioning, and insisted on our accepting, his defects and weaknesses of character as virtues and powers peculiar to himself. Was he indolent, he finds none of the activities which attract or employ the rest of mankind worthy of him. Was he wanting in the qualities that make success, it is success that is contemptible, and not himself that lacks persistency and purpose. Was he poor, money was an unmixed evil. Did his life seem a selfish one, he condemns doing good as one of the weakest of superstitions. To be of use was with him the most killing bait of the wily tempter Uselessness. He had no faculty of generalisation from outside of himself, or at least no experience which would supply the material of such, and he makes his own whim the law, his own range the horizon of the universe. He condemns a world, the hollowness of whose satisfactions he had never had the means of testing, and we recognise Apemantus behind the mask of Timon   He had little active imagination; of the receptive he had much. His appreciation is of the highest quality; his critical power, from want of continuity of mind, very limited and inadequate. He somewhere cites a simile from Ossian, as an example of the superiority of the old poetry to the new, though, even were the historic evidence less convincing, the sentimental melancholy of those poems should be conclusive of their modernness. He had no artistic power such as controls a great work to the serene balance of completeness, but exquisite mechanical skill in the shaping of sentences and paragraphs, or (more rarely) short bits of verse for the expression of a detached thought, sentiment, or image. His works give one the feeling of a sky full of stars—something impressive and exhilarating certainly, something high overhead and freckled thickly with spots of isolated brightness; but whether these have any mutual relation with each other, or have any concern with our mundane matters, is for the most part matter of conjecture—astrology as yet, and not astronomy.

It is curious, considering what Thoreau afterwards became, that he was not by nature an observer. He only saw the things he looked for, and was less poet than naturalist. Till he built his Walden shanty, he did not know that the hickory grew in Concord. Till he went to Maine, he had never seen phosphorescent wood, a phenomenon early familiar to most country boys. At forty he speaks of the seeding of the pine as a new discovery, though

one should have thought that its gold-dust of
blowing pollen might have earlier drawn his eye.
Neither his attention nor his genius was of the
spontaneous kind. He discovered nothing. He
thought everything a discovery of his own, from
moonlight to the planting of acorns and nuts by
squirrels. This is a defect in his character, but one
of his chief charms as a writer. Everything grows
fresh under his hand. He delved in his mind and
nature; he planted them with all manner of native
and foreign seeds, and reaped assiduously. He was
not merely solitary, he would be isolated, and
succeeded at last in almost persuading himself that
he was autochthonous. He valued everything in
proportion as he fancied it to be exclusively his own.
He complains in *Walden*, that there is no one in
Concord with whom he could talk of Oriental
literature, though the man was living within two
miles of his hut who had introduced him to it.
This intellectual selfishness becomes sometimes
almost painful in reading him. He lacked that
generosity of " communication " which Johnson
admired in Burke. De Quincey tells us that Wordsworth was impatient when any one else spoke of
mountains, as if he had a peculiar property in them.
And we can readily understand why it should be
so: no one is satisfied with another's appreciation
of his mistress. But Thoreau seems to have prized
a lofty way of thinking (often we should be inclined
to call it a remote one) not so much because it was
good in itself as because he wished few to share

it with him. It seems now and then as if he did not seek to lure others up "above our lower region of turmoil," but to leave his own name cut on the mountain peak as the first climber. This itch of originality infects his thought and style. To be misty is not to be mystic. He turns commonplaces end for end, and fancies it makes something new of them. As we walk down Park Street, our eye is caught by Dr. Windship's dumb-bells, one of which bears an inscription testifying that it is the heaviest ever put up at arm's length by any athlete; and in reading Mr. Thoreau's books we cannot help feeling as if he sometimes invited our attention to a particular sophism or paradox, as the biggest yet maintained by any single writer. He seeks, at all risks, for perversity of thought, and revives the age of *concetti* while he fancies himself going back to a pre-classical nature. "A day," he says, "passed in the society of those Greek sages, such as described in the *Banquet* of Xenophon, would not be comparable with the dry wit of decayed cranberry-vines and the fresh Attic salt of the moss-beds." It is not so much the True that he loves as the Out-of-the-way. As the Brazen Age shows itself in other men by exaggeration of phrase, so in him by extravagance of statement. He wishes always to trump your suit and to *ruff* when you least expect it. Do you love Nature because she is beautiful? He will find a better argument in her ugliness. Are you tired of the artificial man? He instantly dresses you up an ideal in a Penobscot

Indian, and attributes to this creature of his other-wise-mindedness as peculiarities things that are common to all woodsmen, white or red, and this simply because he has not studied the pale-faced variety.

This notion of an absolute originality, as if one could have a patent-right in it, is an absurdity. A man cannot escape in thought, any more than he can in language, from the past and the present. As no one ever invents a word, and yet language somehow grows by general contribution and necessity, so it is with thought. Mr. Thoreau seems to us to insist in public on going back to flint and steel, when there is a match-box in his pocket which he knows very well how to use at a pinch. Originality consists in power of digesting and assimilating thought, so that they become part of our life and substance. Montaigne, for example, is one of the most original of authors, though he helped himself to ideas in every direction. But they turn to blood and colouring in his style, and give a freshness of complexion that is for ever charming. In Thoreau much seems yet to be foreign and unassimilated, showing itself in symp-toms of indigestion. A preacher-up of Nature, we now and then detect under the surly and stoic garb something of the sophist and the sentimental-iser. We are far from implying that this was conscious on his part. But it is much easier for a man to impose on himself when he measures only with himself. A greater familiarity with ordinary men would have done Thoreau good, by showing him how many fine qualities are common to the race. The radical vice of his theory of life was, that he confounded physical with spiritual remoteness from men. One is far enough withdrawn from his fellows if he keep himself clear of their weaknesses. He is not so truly withdrawn as exiled, if he refuse to share in their strength. " Solitude," says Cowley, " can be well fitted and set right but upon a very few persons. They must have enough knowledge of the world to see the vanity of it, and enough virtue to despise all vanity." It is a morbid self-consciousness that pronounces the world of men empty and worthless before trying it, the instinctive evasion of one who is sensible of some innate weakness, and retorts the accusation of it before any has made it but himself. To a healthy mind, the world is a constant challenge of opportunity. Mr. Thoreau had not a healthy mind, or he would not have been so fond of prescribing. His whole life was a search for the doctor. The old mystics had a wiser sense of what the world was worth. They ordained a severe apprenticeship to law, and even ceremonial, in order to the gaining of freedom and mastery over these. Seven years of service for Rachel were to be rewarded at last with Leah. Seven other years of faithfulness with her were to win them at last the true bride of their souls. Active Life was with them the only path to the Contemplative.

Thoreau had no humour, and this implies that

he was a sorry logician. Himself an artist in rhetoric, he confounds thought with style when he undertakes to speak of the latter. He was for ever talking of getting away from the world, but he must be always near enough to it, nay, to the Concord corner of it, to feel the impression he makes there. He verifies the shrewd remark of Sainte-Beuve, " On touche encore à son temps et très-fort, même quand on le repousse." This egotism of his is a Stylites pillar after all, a seclusion which keeps him in the public eye. The dignity of man is an excellent thing, but therefore to hold one's self too sacred and precious is the reverse of excellent. There is something delightfully absurd in six volumes addressed to a world of such " vulgar fellows " as Thoreau affirmed his fellowmen to be. We once had a glimpse of a genuine solitary who spent his winters one hundred and fifty miles beyond all human communication, and there dwelt with his rifle as his only confidant. Compared with this, the shanty on Walden Pond has something the air, it must be confessed, of the Hermitage of La Chevrette. We do not believe that the way to a true cosmopolitanism carries one into the woods or the society of musquashes. Perhaps the narrowest provincialism is that of Self; that of Kleinwinkel is nothing to it. The natural man, like the singing birds, comes out of the forest as inevitably as the natural bear and the wild-cat stick there. To seek to be natural implies a consciousness that forbids all naturalness for ever. It is as easy—and no easier—to be natural in a *salon* as in a swamp, if one do not aim at it, for what we call unnaturalness always has its spring in a man's thinking too much about himself. "It is impossible," said Turgot, "for a vulgar man to be simple."

We look upon a great deal of the modern sentimentalism about Nature as a mark of disease. It is one more symptom of the general liver-complaint. To a man of wholesome constitution the wilderness is well enough for a mood or a vacation, but not for a habit of life. Those who have most loudly advertised their passion for seclusion and their intimacy with Nature, from Petrarch down, have been mostly sentimentalists, unreal men, misanthropes on the spindle side, solacing an uneasy suspicion of themselves by professing contempt for their kind. They make demands on the world in advance proportioned to their inward measure of their own merit, and are angry that the world pays only by the visible measure of performance. It is true of Rousseau, the modern founder of the sect, true of Saint Pierre, his intellectual child, and of Chateaubriand, his grandchild, the inventor, we might almost say, of the primitive forest, and who first was touched by the solemn falling of a tree from natural decay in the windless silence of the woods. It is a very shallow view that affirms trees and rocks to be healthy, and cannot see that men in communities are just as true to the laws of their organisation and destiny; that can tolerate the puffin and the fox, but not the fool and the knave; that would shun politics because of its demagogues, and snuff up the stench of the obscene fungus. The divine life of Nature is more wonderful, more various, more sublime in man than in any other of her works, and the wisdom that is gained by commerce with men, as Montaigne and Shakespeare gained it, or with one's own soul among men, as Dante, is the most delightful, as it is the most precious, of all. In outward nature it is still man that interests us, and we care far less for the things seen than the way in which poetic eyes like Wordsworth's or Thoreau's see them, and the reflections they cast there. To hear the to-do that is often made over the simple fact that a man sees the image of himself in the outward world, one is reminded of a savage when he for the first time catches a glimpse of himself in a looking-glass. "Venerable child of Nature," we are tempted to say, "to whose science in the invention of the tobacco-pipe, to whose art in the tattooing of thine undegenerate hide not yet enslaved by tailors, we are slowly striving to climb back, the miracle thou beholdest is sold in my unhappy country for a shilling!" If matters go on as they have done, and everybody must needs blab of all the favours that have been done him by roadside and river brink and woodland walk, as if to kiss and tell were no longer treachery, it will be a positive refreshment to meet a man who is as superbly indifferent to Nature as she is to him. By and by we shall have John Smith, of No. 12,

12th Street, advertising that he is not the J. S. who saw a cow-lily on Thursday last, as he never saw one in his life, would not see one if he could, and is prepared to prove an alibi on the day in question.

Solitary communion with Nature does not seem to have been sanitary or sweetening in its influence on Thoreau's character. On the contrary, his letters show him more cynical as he grew older. While he studied with respectful attention the minks and woodchucks, his neighbours, he looked with utter contempt on the august drama of destiny of which his country was the scene, and on which the curtain had already risen. He was converting us back to a state of nature "so eloquently," as Voltaire said of Rousseau, "that he almost persuaded us to go on all fours," while the wiser fates were making it possible for us to walk erect for the first time. Had he conversed more with his fellows, his sympathies would have widened with the assurance that his peculiar genius had more appreciation, and his writings a larger circle of readers, or at least a warmer one, than he dreamed of. We have the highest testimony [1] to the natural sweetness, sincerity, and nobleness of his temper, and in his books an equally irrefragable one to the rare quality of his mind. He was not a strong thinker, but a sensitive feeler. Yet his mind strikes us as cold and wintry in its purity. A light snow has fallen everywhere in which he seems to come on the track

[1] Emerson's, in the Biographical Sketch prefixed to the *Excursions*.

of the shyer sensations that would elsewhere leave
no trace. We think greater compression would
have done more for his fame. A feeling of sameness
comes over us as we read so much. Trifles are
recorded with an over-minute punctuality and
conscientiousness of detail. He records the state
of his personal thermometer thirteen times a day.
We cannot help thinking sometimes of the man who

> Watches, starves, freezes, and sweats
> To learn but catechisms and alphabets
> Of unconcerning things, matters of fact,

and sometimes of the saying of the Persian poet,
that "when the owl would boast, he boasts of
catching mice at the edge of a hole." We could
readily part with some of his affectations. It was
well enough for Pythagoras to say, once for all,
"When I was Euphorbus at the siege of Troy";
not so well for Thoreau to travesty it into "When
I was a shepherd on the plains of Assyria." A naïve
thing said over again is anything but naïve. But
with every exception, there is no writing comparable with Thoreau's in kind, that is comparable
with it in degree where it is best; where it dis-
engages itself, that is, from the tangled roots and
dead leaves of a second-hand Orientalism, and
runs limpid and smooth and broadening as it
runs, a mirror for whatever is grand and lovely
in both worlds.

George Sand says neatly, that "Art is not a
study of positive reality" (*actuality* were the fitter
word), "but a seeking after ideal truth." It would

be doing very inadequate justice to Thoreau if we left it to be inferred that this ideal element did not exist in him, and that too in larger proportion, if less obtrusive, than his Nature-worship. He took Nature as the mountain-path to an ideal world. If the path wind a good deal, if he record too faithfully every trip over a root, if he botanise somewhat wearisomely, he gives us now and then superb outlooks from some jutting crag, and brings us out at last into an illimitable ether, where the breathing is not difficult for those who have any true touch of the climbing spirit. His shanty-life was a mere impossibility, so far as his own conception of it goes, as an entire independency of mankind. The tub of Diogenes had a sounder bottom. Thoreau's experiment actually presupposed all that complicated civilisation which it theoretically abjured. He squatted on another man's land; he borrows an axe; his boards, his nails, his bricks, his mortar, his books, his lamp, his fish-hooks, his plough, his hoe, all turn state's evidence against him as an accomplice in the sin of that artificial civilisation which rendered it possible that such a person as Henry D. Thoreau should exist at all. *Magnis tamen excidit ausis.* His aim was a noble and a useful one, in the direction of " plain living and high thinking." It was a practical sermon on Emerson's text that " things are in the saddle and ride mankind," an attempt to solve Carlyle's problem (condensed from Johnson) of " lessening your denominator." His whole life was a rebuke of the waste and aimlessness of our American luxury, which is an abject enslavement to tawdry upholstery. He had " fine translunary things " in him. His better style as a writer is in keeping with the simplicity and purity of his life. We have said that his range was narrow, but to be a master is to be a master. He had caught his English at its living source, among the poets and prose-writers of its best days; his literature was extensive and recondite; his quotations are always nuggets of the purest ore: there are sentences of his as perfect as anything in the language, and thoughts as clearly crystallised; his metaphors and images are always fresh from the soil; he had watched Nature like a detective who is to go upon the stand; as we read him, it seems as if all out-of-doors had kept a diary and become its own Montaigne; we look at the landscape as in a Claude Lorraine glass; compared with his, all other books of similar aim, even White's *Selborne*, seem dry as a country clergyman's meteorological journal in an old almanac. He belongs with Donne and Browne and Novalis; if not with the originally creative men, with the scarcely smaller class who are peculiar, and whose leaves shed their invisible thought-seed like ferns.

JOHN STUART MILL'S
"AUTOBIOGRAPHY"

By Richard Holt Hutton

THAT this curious volume delineates, on the whole, a man marked by the most earnest devotion to human good, and the widest intellectual sympathies, no one who reads it with any discernment can doubt. But it is both a very melancholy book to read, and one full of moral paradoxes. It is very sad, in the first instance, to read the story of the over-tutored boy, constantly incurring his father's displeasure for not being able to do what by no possibility could he have done, and apparently without any one to love. Mr. James Mill, vivacious talker, and in a narrow way powerful thinker as he was, was evidently as an educator, on his son's own showing, a hard master, anxious to reap what he had not sown, and to gather what he had not strawed, or as that son himself puts it, expecting "effects without causes." Not that the father did not teach the child with all his might, and teach in many respects well; but then he taught the boy far too much, and expected him to learn besides a great deal that he neither taught him nor showed him where to find. The child began Greek at three years old, read a good deal of Plato at seven, and was writing what he flattered himself was "something serious," a history of the Roman Government,—not a popular history, but a constitutional history of Rome,—by the time he was nine years old. He began logic at twelve, went through a "complete course of political economy" at thirteen, including the most intricate points of the theory of currency. He was a constant writer for the *Westminster Review* at eighteen, was editing Bentham's *Theory of Evidence* and writing habitual criticisms of the Parliamentary debates at nineteen. At twenty he fell into a profound melancholy, on discovering that the only objects of life for which he lived,—the objects of social and political reformers,—would, if suddenly and completely granted, give him no happiness whatever. Such a childhood and youth, lived apparently without a single strong affection,—for his relation to his father was one of deep respect and fear, rather than love, and he tells us frankly, in describing the melancholy to which I have alluded, that if he had loved any one well enough to confide in him, the melancholy would not have been,— resulting at the age of eighteen in the production of what Mr. Mill himself says might, with as little extravagance as would ever be involved in the application of such a phrase to a human being, be called "a mere reasoning machine,"—are not pleasant subjects of contemplation, even though it be true, as Mr. Mill asserts, that the over-supply of study and under-supply of love, did not prevent his childhood from being a happy one. Nor are the other personal incidents of the autobiography of a different cast. Nothing is more remarkable than the fewness, limited character, and apparently, so far as close intercourse was concerned, temporary duration, of most of Mr Mill's friendships. The one close and intimate friendship of his life, which made up to him for the insufficiency of all others, that with the married lady who, after the death of her husband, became his wife, was one which for a long time subjected him to slanders, the pain of which his sensitive nature evidently felt very keenly. And yet he must have been aware that though in his own conduct he had kept free from all stain, his example was an exceedingly dangerous and mischievous one for others, who might be tempted by his moral authority to follow in a track in which they would not have had the strength to tread. Add to this that his married life was very brief, only seven years and a half, being unexpectedly cut short, and that his passionate reverence for his wife's memory and genius—in his own words, "a religion"—was one which, as he must have been perfectly sensible, he could not possibly make to appear otherwise than extravagant, not to say an hallucination, in the eyes of the rest of mankind, and yet that he was possessed by an irresistible yearning to attempt to embody it in all the tender and enthusiastic hyperbole of which it is so pathetic to find a man who gained his fame by

his " dry-light " a master, and it is impossible not
to feel that the human incidents in Mr. Mill's
career are very sad.   True, his short service in
Parliament, when he was already advanced in
years, was one to bring him much intellectual
consideration and a certain amount of popularity.
But even that terminated in a defeat, and was
hardly successful enough to repay him for the loss
of literary productiveness which those three years
of practical drudgery imposed.   In spite of the
evident satisfaction and pride with which Mr.
Mill saw that his school of philosophy had gained
rapid ground since the publication of his *Logic*,
and that his large and liberal view of the science
of political economy had made still more rapid
way amongst all classes, the record of his life which
he leaves behind him is not even in its own tone,
and still less in the effect produced on the reader,
a bright and happy one.   It is " sicklied o'er with
the pale cast of thought,"—and of thought that
has to do duty for much, both of feeling and of
action, which usually goes to constitute the full
life of a large mind.

And besides the sense of sadness which the
human incident of the autobiography produces,
the intellectual and moral story itself is full of
paradox which weighs upon the heart as well as
the mind.   Mr. Mill was brought up by his father
to believe that Christianity was false, and that
even as regards natural religion there was no ground
for faith.   How far he retained the latter opinion,

—he evidently did retain the former,—it is understood that some future work will tell us. But in
the meantime, he is most anxious to point out
that religion, in what he thinks the best sense, is
possible even to one who does not believe in God.
That best sense is the sense in which religion stands
for an ideal conception of a Perfect Being to which
those who have such a conception " habitually
refer as the guide of their conscience," an ideal,
he says, " far nearer to perfection than the objective
Deity of those who think themselves obliged to
find absolute goodness in the author of a world
so crowded with suffering and so deformed by
injustice as ours." Unfortunately, however, this
"ideal conception of a perfect Being" is not a
power on which human nature can lean. It is
merely its own best thought of itself; so that it
dwindles when the mind and heart contract, and
vanishes just when there is most need of help. This
Mr. Mill himself felt at one period of his life. At
the age of twenty he underwent a crisis which
apparently corresponded in his own opinion to the
state of mind that leads to "a Wesleyan's con-
version." I wish we could extract in full his eloquent
and impressive description of this rather thin moral
crisis. Here is his description of the first stage:

From the winter of 1821, when first I read Bentham,
and especially from the commencement of the *Westminster Review*, I had what might truly be called an
object in life; to be a reformer of the world. My conception of my own happiness was entirely identified
with this object. The personal sympathies I wished

for were those of fellow-labourers in this enterprise. I endeavoured to pick up as many flowers as I could by the way: but as a serious and permanent personal satisfaction to rest upon, my whole reliance was placed on this; and I was accustomed to felicitate myself on the certainty of a happy life which I enjoyed, through placing my happiness in something durable and distant, in which some progress might be always making, while it could never be exhausted by complete attainment. This did very well for several years, during which the general improvement going on in the world and the idea of myself as engaged with others in struggling to promote it, seemed enough to fill up an interesting and animated existence. But the time came when I awakened from this as from a dream. It was in the autumn of 1826. I was in a dull state of nerves, such as everybody is occasionally liable to; unsusceptible to enjoyment or pleasurable excitement; one of those moods when what is pleasure at other times, becomes insipid or indifferent; the state, I should think, in which converts to Methodism usually are, when smitten by their first "conviction of sin." In this frame of mind it occurred to me to put the question directly to myself: "Suppose that all your objects in life were realised; that all the changes in institutions and opinions which you are looking forward to could be completely effected at this very instant; would this be a great joy and happiness to you?" And an irrepressible self-consciousness distinctly answered, "No!" At this my heart sank within me: the whole foundation on which my life was constructed fell down. All my happiness was to have been found in the continual pursuit of this end. The end had ceased to charm, and how could there ever again be any interest in the means? I seemed to have nothing left to live for. At first I hoped that the cloud would pass away of itself; but it did not. A night's sleep, the sovereign remedy for the smaller vexations of life, had no effect on it. I awoke to a renewed consciousness of the woful fact. I carried it with me into all companies, into all occupations. Hardly anything had power to cause me even a few minutes' oblivion of it. For some months the cloud seemed to grow thicker and thicker. The lines in Coleridge's *Dejection* —I was not then acquainted with them—exactly describe my case:

> A grief without a pang, void, dark and drear,
> A drowsy, stifled, unimpassioned grief,
> Which finds no natural outlet or relief
> In word, or sigh, or tear.

In vain I sought relief from my favourite books; those memorials of past nobleness and greatness from which I had always hitherto drawn strength and animation. I read them now without feeling or with the accustomed feeling *minus* all its charm; and I became persuaded, that my love of mankind, and of excellence for its own sake, had worn itself out. I sought no comfort by speaking to others of what I felt. If I had loved any one sufficiently to make confiding my griefs a necessity, I should not have been in the condition I was.

It is clear that Mr. Mill felt the deep craving for a more permanent and durable source of spiritual life than any which the most beneficent activity spent in patching up human institutions and laboriously recasting the structure of human society, could secure him,—that he himself had a suspicion that, to use the language of a book he had been taught to make light of, his soul was thirsting for God, and groping after an eternal presence, in which he lived and moved and had his being. What is strange and almost burlesque, if it were not so melancholy, is the mode in which this moral crisis culminates. A few tears shed over Marmontel's *Mémoires*, and the fit passed away:

Two lines of Coleridge, in whom alone of all writers I have found a true description of what I felt, were often in my thoughts, not at this time (for I had never read them), but in a later period of the same mental malady:

> Work without hope draws nectar in a sieve,
> And hope without an object cannot live.

In all probability my case was by no means so peculiar as I fancied it, and I doubt not that many others have passed through a similar state; but the idiosyncrasies of my education had given to the general phenomenon a special character, which made it seem the natural effect of causes that it was hardly possible for time to remove. I frequently asked myself, if I could, or if I was bound to go on living, when life must be passed in this manner. I generally answered to myself, that I did not think I could possibly bear it beyond a year. When, however, not more than half that duration of time had elapsed, a small ray of light broke in upon my gloom. I was reading, accidentally, Marmontel's *Mémoires*, and came to the passage which relates his father's death, the distressed position of the family, and the sudden inspiration by which he, then a mere boy, felt and made them feel that he would be everything to them —would supply the place of all that they had lost. A vivid conception of the scene and its feelings came over me, and I was moved to tears. From this moment my burden grew lighter. The oppression of the thought that all feeling was dead within me, was gone. I was no longer hopeless; I was not a stock or a stone. I had still, it seemed, some of the material out of which all worth of character, and all capacity for happiness, are made. Relieved from my ever present sense of irremediable wretchedness, I gradually found that the ordinary incidents of life could again give me some pleasure; that I could again find enjoyment, not intense, but sufficient for cheerfulness, in sunshine and sky, in books, in conversation, in public affairs; and that there was, once more, excitement, though of a moderate kind, in exerting myself for my opinions, and for the public good. Thus the cloud gradually drew off, and I again enjoyed life: and though I had several relapses, some of which lasted many months, I never again was as miserable as I had been.

And the only permanent fruit which this experience left behind it seems to have been curiously slight. It produced a threefold moral result,—first, a grave alarm at the dangerously undermining capacities of his own power of moral analysis, which promised to unravel all those artificial moral webs of painful and pleasurable associations with injurious and useful actions, respectively, which his father had so laboriously woven for him during his childhood and youth; and further, two notable practical conclusions,—one, that in order to attain happiness (which he " never wavered " in regarding as " the test of all rules of conduct and the end of life "), the best strategy is a kind of flank march, —to aim at something else, at some ideal end, not consciously as a means to happiness, but as an end in itself,—so, he held, may you have a better chance of securing happiness by the way, than you can by any direct pursuit of it,—and the other, that it is most desirable to cultivate the feelings, the passive susceptibilities, as well as the reasoning and active powers, if the utilitarian life is to be made enjoyable. Surely a profound sense of the inadequacy of ordinary human success to the cravings of the human spirit was never followed by a less radical moral change. That it resulted in a new breadth of sympathy with writers like Coleridge and Wordsworth, whose fundamental modes of thought and faith Mr. Mill entirely rejected, but for whose modes of sentiment, after this period of his life, he somehow managed, not very intelligibly, to make room, is very true; and it is also true that this lent a new largeness of tone to his writings, and gave him a real superiority in all matters of taste to that of the utilitarian clique to which he had belonged,—results which enormously widened the scope of his influence, and changed him from the mere expositor of a single school of psychology into the thoughtful critic of many different schools. But as far as I can judge, all this new breadth was gained at the cost of a certain haze which, from this time forth, spread itself over his grasp of the first principles which he still professed to hold. He did not cease to be a utilitarian, but he ceased to distinguish between the duty of promoting your own happiness and of promoting anybody else's, and never could make it clear where he found his moral obligation to sacrifice the former to the latter. He still maintained that actions, and not sentiments, are the true subjects of ethical discrimination; but he discovered that there was a significance which he had never before suspected even in sentiments and emotions of which he continued to maintain that the origin was artificial and arbitrary. He did not cease to declaim against the prejudices engendered by the intuitional theory of philosophy, but he made it one of his peculiar distinctions as an Experience-philosopher, that he recommended the fostering of new prepossessions, only distinguished from the prejudices he strove to dissipate by being, in his opinion, harmless, though quite as little based as those in ultimate or objective truth. He maintained as strongly as ever that the character of man is formed by circumstances, but he discovered that the will can act upon circumstances, and so modify its own future capability of willing; and though it is in his opinion circumstances which enable or induce the will thus to act upon circumstances, he thought and taught that this makes all the difference between fatalism and the doctrine of cause and effect as applied to character. After his influx of new light, he remained as strong a democrat as ever, but he ceased to believe in the self-interest principle as universally efficient to produce good government when applied to multitudes, and indeed qualified his democratic theory by an intellectual aristocracy of feeling which to our minds is the essence of exclusiveness. "A person of high intellect," he writes, "should never go into unintellectual society, unless he can enter it as an apostle; yet he is the only person with high objects, who can ever enter it at all." You can hardly have exclusiveness more extreme than that, or a doctrine more strangely out of moral sympathy with the would-be universalism of the

Benthamite theory. In fact, as it seems to me, Mr. Mill's unquestionable breadth of philosophic treatment was gained at the cost of a certain ambiguity which fell over the root-principles of his philosophy, —an ambiguity by which he won for it a more catholic repute than it deserved. The result of the moral crisis through which Mr. Mill passed at the age of twenty may be described briefly, in my opinion, as this,—that it gave him *tastes* far in advance of his philosophy, foretastes in fact of a true philosophy; and that this moral flavour of something truer and wider, served him in place of the substance of anything truer and wider, during the rest of his life.

The part of the *Autobiography* which I like least, though it is, on the whole, that on which I am most at one with Mr. Mill, is the section in which he reviews his short, but thoughtful Parliamentary career. The tone of this portion of the book is too self-important, too minutely egotistic, for the dry and abstract style in which it is told. It adds little to our knowledge of the Parliamentary struggles in which he was engaged, and nothing to our knowledge of any of the actors in them except himself. The best part of the *Autobiography*, except the remarkable and masterly sketch of his father, Mr. James Mill, is the account of the growth of his own philosophic creed in relation to Logic and Political Economy, but this is of course a part only intelligible to the students of his more abstract works.

On the whole, the book will be found, I think, even by Mr. Mill's most strenuous disciples, a dreary one. It shows that in spite of all Mr. Mill's genuine and generous compassion for human misery and his keen desire to alleviate it, his relation to concrete humanity was of a very confined and reserved kind,—one brightened by few personal ties, and those few not, except in about two cases, really hearty ones. The multitude was to him an object of compassion and of genuine beneficence, but he had no pleasure in men, no delight in actual intercourse with this strange, various, homely world of motley faults and virtues. His nature was composed of a few very fine threads, but wanted a certain strength of basis, and the general effect, though one of high and even enthusiastic disinterestedness, is meagre and pallid. His tastes were refined, but there was a want of homeliness about his hopes. He was too strenuously didactic to be in sympathy with man, and too incessantly analytic to throw his burden upon God. There was something overstrained in all that was noblest in him, this excess seeming to be by way of compensation, as it were, for the number of regions of life in which he found little or nothing where other men find so much. He was strangely deficient in humour, which, perhaps, we ought not to regret, for had he had it, his best work would in all probability have been greatly hampered by such a gift. Unique in intellectual ardour and moral disinterestedness, of tender heart and fastidious tastes, though narrow in his range of practical sympathies, his name will long be famous as that of the most wide-minded and generous of political economists, the most disinterested of utilitarian moralists, and the most accomplished and impartial of empirical philosophers. But as a man, there was in him a certain poverty of nature, in spite of the nobleness in him, —a monotonous joylessness, in spite of the hectic sanguineness of his theoretic creed,—a want of genial trust, which spurred on into an almost artificial zeal his ardour for philosophic reconstruction; and these are qualities which will probably put a well-marked limit on the future propagation of an influence such as few writers on such subjects have ever before attained within the period of their own lifetime.

AN ENGLISH GNOSTIC

"THE SPECTATOR," 1867

SOME strange, rather striking, and very reckless papers, full of a sort of blasphemy—we use the word not to convey any censure of ours, but in its strict meaning,—which has scarcely been heard in any tone but that of rebellious passion since the conflict of Christian faith with Paganism first began, have appeared in the *Reader* during the last two weeks, purporting to be "Papers of a Suicide,"—and in the second of the series, termed " A Religious and Autobiographical Romance," — reviving in language that reminds one rather vividly of one of the choruses in Mr. Swinburne's *Atalanta*, where the maidens address " that Supreme evil God," one of the most curious and most utterly obsolete dreams of the oppressed Gnostic imagination. True, there is a hint that the papers are partly, if not altogether dramatic, and that they are supposed to be written by a man with a germ of insanity in his blood; but still this hypothesis would scarcely be resorted to, to give a colour of probability to a very strange form of evil dream, were there not a wish on the part of the writer to revive that intellectual nightmare of an age of religious nightmares, with express

reference to the position of modern faith and un-
belief. The Gnostic fancy to which we refer was,
—that the Jewish Scriptures were inspired by an
inferior and to some extent incapable god,—the
demiurgos, as the Gnostics called him,—who was
the instrument indeed of creating the earth, and of
governing it when created, but whose power was
altogether limited by the matter with which he
had to struggle in the task. We remember a striking
picture, drawn by one of these wild speculators,
which represents the *demiurgos* as sitting in despair
in the dust, and crying out the creative words in
Genesis, " Let Light be," not with the fiat of a
divine will, but in the despairing shriek of entreaty
to a superior power. In this conception of the
Gnostics the Manager of the earth and of nature
was in no sense infinite,—but a finite though
powerful angel, unequal to prevent evil from
creeping into his universe at every pore; and they
proceeded to show how it might be subsequently
removed thence by emanations and manifestations
of the superior divinities above him. It is the first
part only of this grotesque conception which has
been taken up in these strange " Papers of a Suicide."
It is apparently taken up, we will not say with any
serious intent to press it upon the world as true,
but with a kind of reckless pleasure in throwing
out a new suggestion that may swell the chaos of
conflicting irreligions, and that the writer perhaps
seriously thinks has as good a title to acceptance
as any other. At all events, his view is urged with

passion and vehemence, and hideous as it is, it does suggest a question of much interest on which it may be worth while to say a few words,—namely, why it is that in an age of religious anarchy like ours these old Gnostic dreams of deputy-gods, limited deities but half equal to their work, have so entirely vanished, and left no intermediate speculation in the great chasm between the most reverent Theism and blank Atheism. Of the latter there is only too much; yet the marks of personality and design written upon the universe do not disappear when spiritual worship dies out of the heart, and it seems on the first glance strange that men who cannot perceive the divine love, should at once cast away with their belief in that, their belief in a personal power altogether. The imaginary suicide discriminates between the two, and in a passage of curious bitterness revives the old Gnostic theory:

But man cannot avoid hasty generalisations, and Religion is but one of them, after all. Man cannot suspend his opinion of the Designer, and passes from the Supreme Evil of the savage to the Supreme Good of the Jew and the Christian. What if God be as ignorant of the future as ourselves? What if he sits in stupefaction at the flame of life which He has kindled? . . . Let me speak of God as I think I have found him. Let me say, for once, what is in the hearts of many. I find, then, a Designer wondrous powerful, but not omnipotent. I find him more successful in dealing with matter than with life; more successful with life than with mind. I find his incapacity more visible as the scale of creation ascends, until in man even the most religious mourns over the failure. I deduce the conclusion that the maker of the Universe can be no Supreme Being. He seems to me One permitted to fashion the worlds out of a substance given to Him as clay to a child, subject to certain laws which He is incompetent to alter, and which he, like man, can only guide by obeying. I doubt if He foresaw the phenomena of life when he arranged the systems of what we call the Universe. I should feel sure of this were it settled that the earth is the only inhabited planet. Such a being might have power to interfere so that he did not disarrange his own cosmos: he might be unable to make chaos come again. *His* Maker may possibly call him to account one day. Ourselves may be summoned to a greater Bar than even Christians deem of, to bear witness to the wrongs we have suffered at the hands of God. I trace in everything the faults of One who has attempted too much.

That is, in its way, startling enough, and yet we suppose no Western mind, at all events in Christian ages, unless it be the writer's, has ever even glanced at such a view of the creator of our world;—nor, indeed, anybody at all who has found a revelation of any sort in the Old Testament, since the time of the Syrian Gnostics. To suggest, as the supposed suicide elsewhere does, that the Old Testament contains an account of a real revelation from Jehovah to the Jews, but from a Jehovah who, so far from being omnipotent, was compelled from inadequate power to break many of his covenants, and then to find apologies in the conduct of his people for going back from his promises,—carries us off into the theosophic and dæmonological dreams of a vanished world. Why is this so? Why have all intermediate speculations between a perfectly wise and self-existent God, and pure Atheism vanished so completely even from the fancies of men ? Hume no doubt suggested that if God was to be regarded only as the cause of the universe, you must take Him to be a being of mixed good and evil, mixed qualities of every kind, like the effect; but though he threw out this paradox, he never seriously proposed to any one to believe in an imperfect and hampered God. Even the coldest deist is rather inclined in modern days to throw the blame of seeming failures upon either the human will or the human understanding, than to impute them to radical deficiencies in the power or plan of the Creator.

We ascribe the entire disappearance in modern times of all mediate forms of belief between pure theism and pure atheism in some slight degree to the growth of that unity of science which shows us that all matter is force, and that all forces are regulated by a coherent plan and are identical in essence. Thus we are driven to choose between force as itself original, and force as issuing directly from a living Will, the former being blank atheism, the latter omnipotence, or at least so far omnipotence that there are no conceivable external forces to limit the power of Deity which are not sprung from Himself. Thus much the growth of science has done,—it has cleared away all such intermediate conceptions as would attribute certain powers, and deny others, to a subordinate deity like

the Gnostic *demiurgos*,—for it obliges us to trace
back all powers to a well-spring of homogeneous
power, and so contributes greatly to do away with
all intermediate stages, all delegation, of the great
natural forces which lie around the human will.
But this scientific growth of evidence, which
sceptics are the first to admit, against any divided
reign in the realm of nature and of natural power,
would not necessarily exclude various inferences
amongst deists as to the moral nature of God, or
extinguish Hume's suggestion that to the cause of
a universe showing mixed good and evil it would
be only scientific to ascribe mixed good and evil
qualities. But here a very much more powerful
influence comes in. The Christian revelation,
especially the Incarnation, has almost forced men
to choose between two alternatives—to trace back
all power to a divine background of holiness and
love,—or to rest in power as itself final, and as
vouchsafing no self-justification to finite beings
of its righteousness. Until the world had its vision
of the Son of God actually putting off power out
of the depth of divine love in order to manifest that
love in shame and suffering, it was possible for the
human imagination to attribute all varieties or
shades of goodness to the ultimate ruler of the
universe without any feeling of moral contradiction.
But when once we had caught a glimpse of such
graduation in the divine nature as puts love and
righteousness infinitely beyond power,—the latter
being, as it were, an accident that could be put off,

the others an essence that followed even the divine
Son into human conditions of existence,—and when
once the thirst of man for God had been actually
satisfied in such a life as our Lord's, it became
impossible to play, as it were, with the attributes
of God, and vary them in imagination. Men felt
either that the very essence of God was love and
righteousness, and that His power, however great
the mystery of this unintelligible world, was the
mere *arm* of that love, and not His essence; or if
that faith was beyond their grasp, they gave up
altogether thinking of moral distinctions as ultimate
and infinite at all, and made no attempt to trace
a moral character in the unsearchable fountain of
existence. No mind which has ever leaped to the
conviction that ineffable purity and love is at the
origin of all things, could surrender it without
surrendering all belief in the ultimate character
of moral distinctions, without beginning to regard
good and evil, love and malice, as human accidents
which cannot properly be carried up to the source
of life at all. The perplexities still exist,—and have
been stated with horrid force of conception by this
modern Gnostic,—which once induced men to
attribute to the Creator mixed qualities and limited
power to carry those qualities into the work of
creation. But these intermediate modes of thought
between faith and atheism have been burned up
by the mere brightness of the Incarnation. There
is such an infinite difference between the spring
of the heart towards the God who was in Christ,

and towards any other conception man can make
for himself, that if, overpowered by intellectual
perplexities, you reject the one, there is no in-
clination left to subdivide the infinite distance
between the God incarnate in Christ, and the God
whose essence is power, on whom the mere deist
falls back. Of course we do not mean that all who
reject the Incarnation fall back on such a God, for
Christ has won over the greater part of our modern
Theism to that type which the surrender by Christ
of His power for the work of love first gave it. But
however men call themselves, the Christian revelation has really forced us into the alternative
between a worship of holiness and love as wielding
the divine power, and the exchange of all true
worship for mere acquiescence in immutable decrees.
Between these two extremes there is now no resting-
place for the mind. An intermediate Gnosticism,
such as the supposed suicide puts forth, could never
be possible again, unless Christ could be forgotten.

ABOUT RYMER AND HIS "FŒDERA"

"THE ATHENÆUM," 1869

ON what strange chances great results depend! If Rymer's father had not been hanged, the world would never have possessed Rymer's *Fœdera*. Utilitarians would perhaps say that we should be glad of what was suffered by the father at the gallows, in proportion with what the son collected and transcribed in the old Chapter-House at Westminster. We are sorry for the sire; but our sympathy is a little diminished by the fact that the son seems to have borne his father's hanging with that philosophy with which Rochefoucauld says every man bears the calamities which fall on his friends and neighbours.

Rymer and his *Fœdera* are known—or rather Rymer's *Fœdera* is known—all over the civilised world. There is not an historical writer in Europe and America who has not to go often and drink deeply at that fountain-head of history. There is not an historical student in any part of the globe who is not, in some way or other, interested in this collection of documents. When the *Fœdera* appeared, the Muse of History shook off her drowsiness, tightened her sandals, drew her girdle closer,

and started on a new path. Since that period, the
goodly tomes in which the collection is printed
have been the treasures of all libraries; but little
or nothing has been known of the author. So far,
general readers whose languid eyes fall on the
words "Rymer: *Fœd.*," at the tail of a note, know
nothing more of author or book than they saw in
those words themselves.

Now, Sir Thomas Duffus Hardy has come
forward to do what he has so often done before,
—to instruct and interest the public. On this
occasion, the subject is Rymer and the *Fœdera*.
Sir Thomas has just published the first volume of
a *Syllabus* (in English) *of the Documents relating
to England and other Kingdoms contained in the
Collection known as "Rymer's Fœdera."* That is
to say, that every document in the original ponderous
collection is here described, as to its contents, in
a few clear and concise phrases. The gratitude
which the world owed to Rymer, or to Halifax and
Somers, with whom the idea of making such a
collection seems to have originated, will, in perhaps
greater measure, be paid to the Deputy-Keeper
of the Public Records. We say in greater measure,
because, when complete, the *Syllabus* will give
to every man the concentrated essence of the
original mass, and because Sir Thomas has added
an account of the author which, for the first time,
places him bodily, and full of quaint old life, in
presence of the reader.

We have said that Thomas Rymer's father,

Ralph, was hanged. Ralph was a Yorkshire gentleman of some substance, and of such hot Republican
principles that confiscated Royalist estates fell to
him by way of encouragement. The Restoration
deprived him of what he had thus earned, and also
of nearly all that he had inherited; and this sent
Ralph Rymer and his eldest son Ralph, with the
swords and pistols that were left to them, into the
" Presbyterian rising " of 1663. It was all crushed
in one night, and among the many prisoners sen-
tenced to be hanged, drawn and quartered, Ralph
Rymer was one. " Exequandus apud *Leeds*," or
elsewhere, was the euphuism then for putting a
man through that direful process. The eldest son,
accomplice of the father, was liberated from prison
only when death threatened to be his emancipator.

Thomas Rymer, the Fœderalist, if we may so
call him, happened to have for schoolmaster one
Smelt, at Danby Wisk, who was what Sir Thomas
Hardy calls a " Loyalist," but what Parliament-
arians would have called a " Royalist." In the
hottest time of the Commonwealth he contrived
to teach his boys Royalistic principles, something
after the fashion of Bishop Dupanloup, of Orleans,
who, with the Emperor Louis Napoleon and the
Empress Eugénie in his mind, remarked how very
superior Pilate's wife was to Pilate!

Dealing in the above way with rebels and regi-
cides, Smelt's precepts seem to have had more
influence on Thomas Rymer's mind than his
father's principles and practice. He passed to

Cambridge, thence to Gray's Inn, and subsequently
into the world, as a poor, ill-fed, and worse paid
author. He is best remembered for his rhymed
tragedy, licensed in 1677, *Edgar; or, the English
Monarch*. It was avowedly written in support of
a system, for attempting to overthrow which the
author's father had been hanged, drawn and quartered, and his family all but beggared. The play
pleased nobody; but Rymer was convinced that
the public lacked judgment. He failed even more
as a critic than as a writer. He could not even
happily imitate the ancients whom he praised. He
abused Fletcher, assailed Shakespeare as something
between a beast and a barbarian, and referred to
Milton as the author of a thing which some people
were pleased to call a poem! Macaulay says Rymer
was "the worst critic that ever lived." What he
was as a dramatic author may be described in the
words of a piece which, not long before Rymer
wrote his *Edgar*, had been played and damned,—
Arrowsmith's *Reformation*. "Does he ever write
himself?" asks one of the characters. "Yes, yes,"
is the reply; "but, as all your professed critics
do, damnably ill."

Nevertheless, the beggared Yorkshireman continued to ply his pen, eulogising crowned pates
and pelting the poets. He had touched everything
and had not adorned much, when, in 1692, he
succeeded Shadwell as Historiographer Royal.
Half-a-dozen years or so before, Rymer had criti-
cised even this official, asserting that he never wrote

truth except by chance, and that the whole herd of royal historigraphers were, in fact, little better than asses, both ignorant and malicious. Eight months later, Rymer was appointed to collect and edit unpublished records, the collection which grew into the shape and form in which we now have it by the help of other editors. The publication served many a purpose; among others, it buoyed difficult straits for the safe passage of fresh navigators on historical seas; and it illumined the waste of waters over which old navigators of that sort had tossed and tumbled, and had then scrambled shoreward with small salvage of the precious freight of truth. Rymer was the new pilot and explorer. Fancy the savage delight of the amiable creatures who envied him his appointment, when they discovered that the apparently most important document with which he started was a forgery! If he had detected and exposed it, the same men would probably have tried to lessen the credit of the detection: perhaps they would have faintly suggested the genuineness of the paper itself.

Be this as it may, the *Fœdera* became the work, delight and torture of Rymer's life. Hitherto, with rare exceptions, Government had discouraged the publication of any political or State records. Now, a certain class of them were given up to Rymer to print and spread abroad in ponderous volumes. It turned the eyes of the historic world on him and his labours. Scholars at home and abroad became his friends and correspondents. His slip at starting did not ruin him, as such a man's good-natured friends would take care it should do now. Rymer's love for his work grew with its progress. He lived with his transcribers amid actual book-worms; and shook them out with the dust in which they lived and housed, from records which had not been read since the clerks drew, and high-contracting parties signed them. The explorer was ill paid, grudgingly paid, sometimes not paid at all for his work. Out of his small salary as Historiographer he furnished the wages of his clerks and the cost of his materials. He trusted to the honour of the Government to reimburse him; but that honour seems to have been of a very easy nature, sometimes doling, at others denying. The whole history of Rymer amid the records is a new and delightful chapter in *The Curiosities of Literature*. When this Herculean editor had put forth fifteen volumes, and had collected materials for a sixteenth, he died one December day in 1713, in Arundel Street, Strand, and three days after he was buried in the Church of St. Clement Danes. His work was continued by Saunderson. All readers who are curious in the matter have now only to consult the *Syllabus*, with its at once masterly and amusing Preface, by Sir Thomas Duffus Hardy. They will there learn all that can now be known about Rymer and his *Fœdera*.

WALTER SAVAGE LANDOR

By Algernon Charles Swinburne

Walter Savage Landor, born at Warwick, January 30th, 1775, died at Florence, September 17th, 1864. In the course of this long life he had won for himself such a double crown of glory in verse and in prose as has been worn by no other Englishman but Milton. And with that special object of his lifelong veneration he had likewise in common other claims upon our reverence to which no third competitor among English poets can equally pretend. He had the same constancy to the same principles, the same devotion to the same ideal of civic and heroic life; the same love, the same loyalty, the same wrath, scorn, and hatred, for the same several objects respectively; the same faith in the example and kinship to the spirit of the republican Romans, the same natural enjoyment and mastery of their tongue. Not accident merely but attraction must in any case have drawn them to enlist in the ranks and serve under the standard of the ancient Latin army of patriots and poets. But to Landor even more than to Milton the service of the Roman Muse was a natural and necessary expression of his genius, a spontaneous and just direction of its full and exuberant forces. At the age of twenty he published an eloquent vindication of her claims upon the service and devotion of modern writers—the first sketch or suggestion of a longer essay, to be published in its final form just fifty-two years later. In 1795 appeared in a small volume, "divided into three books," *The Poems of Walter Savage Landor*, and, in pamphlet form of nineteen pages, an anonymous *Moral Epistle, respectfully dedicated to Earl Stanhope*. No poet at the age of twenty ever had more vigour of style and fluency of verse; nor perhaps has any ever shown such masterly command of epigram and satire, made vivid and vital by the purest enthusiasm and most generous indignation. Three years later appeared the first edition of the first great work which was to inscribe his name for ever among the great names in English poetry. The second edition of *Gebir* appeared in 1803, with a text corrected of grave errors and improved by magnificent additions. About the same time the whole poem was also published in a Latin form, which for might and melody of line, for power and perfection of language, must always dispute the palm of precedence with the English version. In 1808, under an impulse not less heroic than that which was afterwards to lead Byron to a glorious death in redemption of Greece and his own good fame, Landor, then aged thirty-three, left England for Spain as a volunteer to serve in the national army against Napoleon at the head of a regiment raised and supported at his sole expense. After some three months' campaigning came the affair of Cintra and its disasters; "his troop," in the words of his biographer, "dispersed or melted away, and he came back to England in as great a hurry as he had left it," but bringing with him the honourable recollection of a brave design unselfishly attempted, and the material in his memory for the sublimest poem published in our language between the last masterpiece of Milton and the first masterpiece of Shelley—one equally worthy to stand unchallenged beside either for poetic perfection as well as moral majesty— the lofty tragedy of *Count Julian*, which appeared in 1812, without the name of its author. No comparable work is to be found in English poetry between the date of *Samson Agonistes* and the date of *Prometheus Unbound*; and with both these great works it has some points of greatness in common. The superhuman isolation of agony and endurance which encircles and exalts the hero is in each case expressed with equally appropriate magnificence of effect. The style of *Count Julian*, if somewhat deficient in dramatic ease and the fluency of natural dialogue, has such might and purity and majesty of speech as elsewhere we find only in Milton so long and so steadily sustained.

In May 1811 Landor had suddenly married Miss Julia Thuillier, with whose looks he had fallen in love at first sight in a ball-room at Bath; and in June they settled for awhile at Llanthony

Abbey in Wales, from whence he was worried in three years' time by the combined vexation of neighbours and tenants, lawyers and lords-lieutenant; not before much toil and money had been nobly wasted on attempts to improve the sterility of the land, to relieve the wretchedness and raise the condition of the peasantry. He left England for France at first, but after a brief residence at Tours took up his abode for three years at Como; "and three more wandering years he passed," says his biographer, "between Pisa and Pistoja, before he pitched his tent in Florence in 1821." In 1824 appeared the first series of his *Imaginary Conversations*; in 1826 "the second edition, corrected and enlarged": a supplementary third volume was added in 1828; and in 1829 the second series was given to the world. Not until 1846 was a fresh instalment added, in the second volume of his collected and selected works. During the interval he had published his three other most famous and greatest books in prose: *The Citation and Examination of William Shakespeare*, 1834; *Pericles and Aspasia*, 1836; *The Pentameron*, 1837. To the last of these was originally appended *The Pentalogia*, containing five of the very finest among his shorter studies in dramatic poetry. In 1847 he published his most important Latin work, *Poemata et Inscriptiones*, comprising, with large additions, the main contents of two former volumes of idyllic, satiric, elegiac, and lyric verse; and in the same golden year of his poetic life appeared the very crown and flower of its manifold labours, *The Hellenics of Walter Savage Landor*, enlarged and completed. Twelve years later this book was reissued, with additions of more or less value, with alterations generally to be regretted, and with omissions invariably to be deplored. In 1853 he put forth *The Last Fruit off an Old Tree*, containing fresh conversations, critical and controversial essays, miscellaneous epigrams, lyrics, and occasional poems of various kind and merit, closing with *Five Scenes* on the martyrdom of Beatrice Cenci, unsurpassed even by their author himself for noble and heroic pathos, for subtle and genial, tragic and profound, ardent and compassionate insight into character, with consummate mastery of dramatic and spiritual truth. In 1856 he published *Antony and Octavius—Scenes for the Study*, twelve consecutive poems in dialogue which alone would suffice to place him high among the few great masters of historic drama. In 1858 appeared a metrical miscellany bearing the title of *Dry Sticks Fagoted by W. S. Landor*, and containing among other things graver and lighter certain epigrammatic and satirical attacks which reinvolved him in the troubles of an action for libel; and in July of the same year he returned for the last six years of his life to Italy, which he had left for England in 1835. Embittered and distracted by domestic dissensions, if brightened and relieved by the affection and veneration of friends and strangers, this final period of his troubled and splendid career came at last to a quiet end on the 17th (as aforesaid) of September, 1864. In the preceding year he had published a last volume of *Heroic Idyls, with additional poems,* English and Latin; the better part of them well worthy to be indeed the " last fruit " of a genius which after a life of eighty-eight years had lost nothing of its majestic and pathetic power, its exquisite and exalted loveliness.

A complete list of Landor's writings, published or privately printed, in English, Latin, and Italian, including pamphlets, fly-sheets, and occasional newspaper correspondence on political or literary questions, it would be difficult to give anywhere and impossible to give here. From nineteen almost to ninety his intellectual and literary activity was indefatigably incessant; but, herein at least like Charles Lamb, whose cordial admiration he so cordially returned, he could not write a note of three lines which did not bear the mark of his " Roman hand " in its matchless and inimitable command of a style at once the most powerful and the purest of his age. The one charge which can ever seriously be brought and maintained against it is that of such occasional obscurity or difficulty as may arise from excessive strictness in condensation of phrase and expurgation of matter not always superfluous, and sometimes almost indispensable. His English prose and his Latin verse are perhaps more frequently and more gravely liable to this charge than either his English verse or his Latin prose. At times it is well-nigh

impossible for an eye less keen and swift, a scholarship less exquisite and ready than his own, to catch
the precise direction and follow the perfect course
of his rapid thought and radiant utterance. This
apparently studious pursuit and preference of the
most terse and elliptic expression which could be
found for anything he might have to say could not
but occasionally make even so sovereign a master
of two great languages appear " dark with excess
of light "; but from no former master of either
tongue in prose or verse was ever the quality of
real obscurity, of loose and nebulous incertitude,
more utterly alien or more naturally remote. There
is nothing of cloud or fog about the path on which
he leads us; but we feel now and then the want
of a bridge or a handrail; we have to leap from
point to point of narrative or argument without
the usual help of a connecting plank. Even in his
dramatic works, where least of all it should have
been found, this lack of visible connection or
sequence in details of thought or action is too often
a source of sensible perplexity. In his noble trilogy
on the history of Giovanna Queen of Naples it is
sometimes actually difficult to realise on a first
reading what has happened or is happening, or how,
or why, or by what agency—a defect alone sufficient,
but unhappily sufficient in itself, to explain the too
general ignorance of a work so rich in subtle and
noble treatment of character, so sure and strong
in its grasp and rendering of " high actions and
high passions," so rich in humour and in pathos,

so royally serene in its commanding power upon the tragic mainsprings of terror and of pity. As a poet, he may be said on the whole to stand midway between Byron and Shelley,—about as far above the former as below the latter. If we except Catullus and Simonides, it might be hard to match and it would be impossible to overmatch the flawless and blameless yet living and breathing beauty of his most perfect elegies, epigrams, or epitaphs. As truly as prettily was he likened by Leigh Hunt " to a stormy mountain pine which should produce lilies." His passionate compassion, his bitter and burning pity for all wrongs endured in all the world, found only their natural and inevitable outlet in his life-long defence or advocacy of tyrannicide as the last resource of baffled justice, the last discharge of heroic duty. His tender and ardent love of children, of animals, and of flowers, makes fragrant alike the pages of his writing and the records of his life. He was as surely the most gentle and generous as the most headstrong and hot-headed of heroes or of men. Nor ever was any man's best work more thoroughly imbued and informed with evidence of his noblest qualities. His loyalty and liberality of heart were as inexhaustible as his bounty and beneficence of hand. Praise and encouragement, deserved or undeserved, came yet more readily to his lips than challenge or defiance. Reviled and ridiculed by Lord Byron, he retorted on the offender living less readily and less warmly than he lamented and extolled him dead. On the noble dramatic works of his brother Robert he lavished a magnificence of sympathetic praise which his utmost self-estimate would never have exacted for his own. Age and the lapse of time could neither heighten nor lessen the fullness of this rich and ready generosity. To the poets of his own and of the next generation he was not readier to do honour than to those of a later growth, and not seldom of deserts far lower and far lesser claims than theirs. That he was not unconscious of his own, and avowed it with the frank simplicity of nobler times, is not more evident or more certain than that in comparison with his friends and fellows he was liable rather to undervalue than to overrate himself. He was a classic, and no formalist; the wide range of his just and loyal admiration had room for a genius so far from classical as Blake's. Nor in his own highest mood or method of creative as of critical work was he a classic only, in any narrow or exclusive sense of the term. On either side, immediately or hardly below his mighty masterpiece of *Pericles and Aspasia,* stand the two scarcely less beautiful and vivid studies of mediæval Italy and Shakespearean England. The very finest flower of his immortal dialogues is probably to be found in the single volume comprising only "Imaginary Conversations of Greeks and Romans"; his utmost command of passion and pathos may be tested by its transcendent success in the distilled and concentrated tragedy of *Tiberius and Vipsania,* where for once he shows a quality more proper to romantic than classical imagination—the subtle and sublime and terrible power to enter the dark vestibule of distraction, to throw the whole force of his fancy, the whole fire of his spirit, into the "shadowing passion" (as Shakespeare calls it) of gradually imminent insanity. Yet, if this and all other studies from ancient history or legend could be subtracted from the volume of his work, enough would be left whereon to rest the foundation of a fame which time could not sensibly impair.

NOTES ON LEONARDO DA VINCI

By Walter Pater

In Vasari's life of Leonardo da Vinci as we now
read it there are some variations from the first
edition. There, the painter who has fixed the
outward type of Christ for succeeding centuries
was a bold speculator, holding lightly by other
men's beliefs, setting philosophy above Christianity.
Words of his, trenchant enough to justify this
impression, are not recorded, and would have
been out of keeping with a genius of which one
characteristic is a tendency to lose itself in a refined
and graceful mystery. The suspicion was but the
time-honoured form in which the world stamps
its appreciation of one who has thoughts for himself
alone, his high indifferentism, his intolerance of
the common forms of things; and in the second
edition the image was changed into something
fainter and more conventional. But it is still by
a certain mystery in his work, and something
enigmatical beyond the usual measure of great
men, that he fascinates, or perhaps half repels.
His life is one of sudden revolts, with intervals
in which he works not at all, or apart from the
main scope of his work. By a strange fortune the

works on which his more popular fame rested
disappeared early from the world, as the Battle
of the Standard; or are mixed obscurely with the
work of meaner hands, as the Last Supper. His
type of beauty is so exotic that it fascinates a larger
number than it delights, and seems more than that
of any other artist to reflect ideas and views and
some scheme of the world within, so that he seemed
to his contemporaries to be the possessor of some
unsanctified and secret wisdom, as to Michelet
and others to have anticipated modern ideas. He
trifles with his genius, and crowds all his chief
work into a few tormented years of later life; yet
he is so possessed by his genius that he passes un-
moved through the most tragic events, overwhelming
his country and friends, like one who comes across
them by chance on some secret errand.

His *legend*, as the French say, with the anecdotes
which every one knows, is one of the most brilliant
in Vasari. Later writers merely copied it, until,
in 1804, Carlo Amoretti applied to it a criticism
which left hardly a date fixed, and not one of those
anecdotes intact. And now a French writer, M.
Arsène Houssaye, gathering all that is known
about Leonardo in an easily accessible form, has
done for the third of the three great masters what
Grimm has done for Michael Angelo, and Passa-
vant, long since, for Raffaelle. Antiquarianism
has no more to do. For others remain the editing
of the thirteen books of his manuscripts, and the
separation by technical criticism of what in his

reputed works is really his, from what is only half his or the work of his pupils. But a lover of strange souls may still analyse for himself the impression made on him by those works, and try to reach through it a definition of the chief elements of Leonardo's genius. The Legend, corrected and enlarged by its critics, may now and then intervene to support the results of this analysis.

His life has three divisions,—thirty years at Florence, nearly twenty years at Milan, then nineteen years of wandering, till he sinks to rest under the protection of Francis I. at the Château de Clou. The dishonour of illegitimacy hangs over his birth. Piero Antonio, his father, was of a noble Florentine house, of Vinci in the Val d'Arno, and Leonardo, brought up delicately among the true children of that house, was the love-child of his youth, with the keen puissant nature such children often have. We see him in his youth fascinating all men by his beauty, improvising music and songs, buying the caged birds and setting them free as he walked the streets of Florence, fond of odd bright dresses and spirited horses.

From his earliest years he designed many objects, and constructed models in relief, of which Vasari mentions some of women smiling. Signor Piero, thinking over this promise in the child, took him to the workshop of Andrea del Verrocchio, then the most famous artist in Florence. Beautiful objects lay about there,—reliquaries, pyxes, silver

images for the Pope's chapel at Rome, strange
fancy work of the Middle Age keeping odd company with fragments of antiquity, then but lately
discovered. Another student Leonardo may have
seen there—a boy into whose soul the level light
and aërial illusions of Italian sunsets had passed,
in after days famous as Perugino. Verrocchio was
an artist of the earlier Florentine type, carver,
painter, and worker in metals in one; designer,
not of pictures only, but of all things for sacred or
household use, drinking-vessels, ambries, instruments of music, making them all fair to look upon,
filling the common ways of life with the reflection
of some far-off brightness; and years of patience
had refined his hand till his work was now sought
after from distant places.

It happened that Verrocchio was employed by
the brethren of Vallombrosa to paint the Baptism
of Christ, and Leonardo was allowed to finish an
angel in the left-hand corner. It was one of those
moments in which the progress of a great thing—
here that of the art of Italy—presses hard and
sharp on the happiness of an individual, through
whose discouragement and decrease humanity, in
more fortunate persons, comes a step nearer to
its final success.

For beneath the cheerful exterior of the mere
well-paid craftsman, chasing brooches for the copes
of Santa Maria Novella, or twisting metal screens
for the tombs of the Medici, lay the ambitious
desire of expanding the destiny of Italian art by

a larger knowledge and insight into things—a purpose in art not unlike Leonardo's still unconscious purpose; and often, in the modelling of drapery, or of a lifted arm, or of hair cast back from the face, there came to him something of the freer manner and richer humanity of a later age. But in this Baptism the pupil had surpassed the master; and Verrocchio turned away as one stunned, and as if his sweet earlier work must thereafter be distasteful to him, from the bright animated angel of Leonardo's hand.

The angel may still be seen in Florence, a space of sunlight in the cold, laboured old picture; but the legend is true only in sentiment, for painting had always been the art by which Verrocchio set least store. And as in a sense he anticipates Leonardo, so to the last Leonardo recalls the studio of Verrocchio, in the love of beautiful toys, such as the vessel of water for a mirror and lovely needlework about the implicated hands in the Modesty and Vanity, and of reliefs, like those cameos which in The Virgin of the Balances hang all round the girdle of St. Michael, and of bright variegated stones, such as the agates in the Saint Anne, and in a hieratic preciseness and grace, as of a sanctuary swept and garnished. Amid all the cunning and intricacy of his Lombard manner this never left him. Much of it there must have been in that lost picture of Paradise, which he prepared as a cartoon for tapestry to be woven in the looms of Flanders. It was the apex of the older

Florentine style of miniature painting, with patient putting of each leaf upon the trees and each flower in the grass, where the first man and woman were standing.

And because it was the perfection of that style, it awoke in Leonardo some seed of discontent which lay in the secret places of his nature. For the way to perfection is through a series of disgusts; and this picture—all that he had done so far in his life at Florence—was after all in the old slight manner. His art, if it was to be something in the world, must be weighted with more of the meaning of nature and purpose of humanity. Nature was "the true mistress of higher intelligences." So he plunged into the study of nature. And in doing this he followed the manner of the older students; he brooded over the hidden virtues of plants and crystals, the lines traced by the stars as they moved in the sky, over the correspondences which exist between the different orders of living things, through which, to eyes opened, they interpret each other; and for years he seemed to those about him as one listening to a voice silent for other men.

He learned here the art of going deep, of tracking the sources of expression to their subtlest retreats, the power of an intimate presence in the things he handled. He did not at once or entirely break with art; only he was no longer the cheerful objective painter, through whose soul, as through clear glass, the bright figures of Florentine life,

only made a little mellower and more pensive by
the transit, passed on to the white wall. He wasted
many days in curious tricks of design, seeming to
lose himself in the spinning of intricate devices of
lines and colours. He was smitten with a love of
the impossible—the perforation of mountains,
changing the course of rivers, raising great buildings,
such as Giovanni Church, in the air; all those
feats for the performance of which natural magic
professes to have the key. Later writers, indeed,
see in these efforts an anticipation of modern
mechanics; in him they were rather dreams,
thrown off by the overwrought and labouring
brain. Two ideas were especially fixed in him, as
reflexes of things that had touched his brain in
childhood beyond the measure of other impressions—the smiling of women and the motion
of great waters.

And in such studies some interfusion of the
extremes of beauty and terror shaped itself, as an
image that might be seen and touched, in the mind
of this gracious youth, so fixed, that for the rest
of his life it never left him; and as catching glimpses
of it in the strange eyes or hair of chance people,
he would follow such about the streets of Florence
till the sun went down, of whom many sketches
of his remain. Some of these are full of a curious
beauty, that remote beauty apprehended only by
those who have sought it carefully; who, starting
with acknowledged types of beauty, have refined
as far upon these as these refine upon the world

of common forms. But mingled inextricably with this there is an element of mockery also; so that, whether in sorrow or scorn, he caricatures Dante even. Legions of grotesques sweep under his hand; for has not nature, too, her grotesques— the rent rock, the distorting light of evening on lonely roads, the unveiled structure of man in the embryo or the skeleton?

All these swarming fancies unite in the Medusa of the Uffizi Vasari's story of an earlier Medusa, painted on a wooden shield, is perhaps an invention; and yet, properly told, has more of the air of truth about it than anything else in the whole legend. For its real subject is not the serious work of a man, but the experiment of a child. The lizards and glow-worms and other strange small creatures which haunt an Italian vineyard bring before one the whole picture of a child's life in a Tuscan dwelling, half castle, half farm; and are as true to nature as the pretended astonishment of the father for whom the boy has prepared a surprise. It was not in play that he painted that other Medusa, the one great picture which he felt behind him in Florence. The subject has been treated in various ways; Leonardo alone cuts to its centre; he alone realises it as the head of a corpse, exercising its power through all the circumstances of death. What we may call the fascination of corruption penetrates in every touch its exquisitely-finished beauty. About the dainty lines of the cheek a rabbit creeps unheeded. The delicate snakes seem

literally strangling each other in terrified struggle
to escape from the Medusa brain. The hue which
violent death always brings with it is in the features
—features singularly massive and grand, as we
catch them inverted, in a dexterous foreshortening,
sloping upwards, almost sliding down upon us,
crown foremost, like a great calm stone against
which the wave of serpents breaks. But it is
a subject that may well be left to the beautiful
verses of Shelley.

The science of that age was all divination,
clairvoyance, unsubjected to our exact modern
formulas, seeking in an instant of vision to con-
centrate a thousand experiences. Later writers,
thinking only of the well-ordered treatise on
painting which a Frenchman, Raffaelle du Fresne,
a hundred years after, compiled from Leonardo's
bewildered manuscripts, written strangely, as his
manner was, from right to left, have imagined a
rigid order in his inquiries. But such rigid order
was little in accordance with the restlessness of
his character; and if we think of him as the mere
reasoner who subjects design to anatomy, and composition to mathematical rules, we shall hardly
have of him that impression which those about him
received from him. Poring over his crucibles,
making experiments with colour, trying by a
strange variation of the alchemist's dream to discover the secret, not of an elixir to make man's
natural life immortal, but rather of giving immortality to the subtlest and most delicate effects

of painting, he seemed to them rather the sorcerer or the magician, possessed of curious secrets and a hidden knowledge, living in a world of which he alone possessed the key. What his philosophy seems to have been most like is that of Paracelsus or Cardan; and much of the spirit of the older alchemy still hangs about it, with its confidence in short cuts and odd by-ways to knowledge. To him philosophy was to be something giving strange swiftness and double sight, divining the sources of springs beneath the earth or of expression beneath the human countenance, clairvoyant of occult gifts in common or uncommon things, in the reed at the brook-side or the star which draws near to us but once in a century. How in this way the clear purpose was overclouded, the fine chaser's hand perplexed, we but dimly see; the mystery which at no point quite lifts from Leonardo's life is thickest here. But it is certain that at one period of his life he had almost ceased to be an artist.

The year 1483—year of the birth of Raffaelle and the thirty-first of Leonardo's life—is fixed as the date of his visit to Milan by the letter in which he recommends himself to Ludovico Sforza, and offers to tell him for a price strange secrets in the art of war. It was that Sforza who murdered his young nephew by slow poison, yet was so susceptible to religious impressions that he turned his worst passions into a kind of religious cultus, and who took for his device the mulberry tree—

symbol, in its long delay and sudden yielding of flowers and fruit together, of a wisdom which economises all forces for an opportunity of sudden and sure effect. The fame of Leonardo had gone before him, and he was to model a colossal statue of Francesco, the first duke. As for Leonardo himself, he came not as an artist at all, or careful of the fame of one; but as a player on the harp—strange harp of silver of his own construction, shaped in some curious likeness to a horse's skull. The capricious spirit of Ludovico was susceptible to the charm of music, and Leonardo's nature had a kind of spell in it. Fascination is always the word descriptive of him. No portrait of his youth remains; but all tends to make us believe that up to this time some charm of voice and aspect, strong enough to balance the disadvantage of his birth, had played about him. His physical strength was great; it was said that he could bend a horse-shoe like a coil of lead.

The Duomo, work of artists from beyond the Alps, so fantastic to a Florentine used to the mellow, unbroken surfaces of Giotto and Arnolfo, was then in all its freshness; and below, in the streets of Milan, moved a people as fantastic, changeful, and dreamlike. To Leonardo least of all men could there be anything poisonous in the exotic flowers of sentiment which grew there. It was a life of exquisite amusements—Leonardo became a celebrated designer of pageants—and brilliant sins; and it suited the quality of his genius, composed in almost equal parts of curiosity and the desire of beauty, to take things as they came.

Curiosity and the desire of beauty! They are the two elementary forces in Leonardo's genius; curiosity often in conflict with the desire of beauty, but generating, in union with it, a type of subtle and curious grace.

The movement of the thirteenth century was twofold: partly the Renaissance, partly also the coming of what is called the modern spirit, with its realism, its appeal to experience; it comprehended a return to antiquity, and a return to nature. Raffaelle represents the return to antiquity, and Leonardo the return to nature. In this return to nature he was seeking to satisfy a boundless curiosity by her perpetual surprises, a microscopic sense of finish by her finesse, or delicacy of operation, that *subtilitas naturæ* which Bacon notices. So we find him often in intimate relations with men of science, with Fra Luca Paccioli the mathematician, and the anatomist Marc Antonio della Torre. His observations and experiments fill thirteen volumes of manuscript; and those who can judge describe him as anticipating long before, by rapid intuition, the later ideas of science. He explained the obscure light of the unilluminated part of the moon, knew that the sea had once covered the mountains which contain shells, and the gathering of the equatorial waters above the polar.

He who thus penetrated into the most secret parts of nature preferred always the more to the less remote, what, seeming exceptional, was an instance of law more refined, the construction about things of a peculiar atmosphere and mixed lights. He paints flowers with such curious felicity that different writers have attributed to him a fondness for particular flowers, as Clement the cyclamen, and Rio the jasmine; while at Venice there is a stray leaf from his portfolio dotted all over with studies of violets and the wild rose. In him first appears the taste for what is *bizarre* or *recherché* in landscape—hollow places full of the green shadow of bituminous rocks, ridged reefs of trap-rock which cut the water into quaint sheets of light—their exact antitype is in our own western seas—all solemn effects of moving water; you may follow it springing from its distant source among the rocks on the heath of the Madonna of the Balances, passing as a little fall into the treacherous calm of the Madonna of the Lake, next, as a goodly river below the cliffs of the Madonna of the Rocks, washing the white walls of its distant villages, stealing out in a network of divided streams in La Gioconda to the sea-shore of the Saint Anne, —that delicate place, where the wind passes like the hand of some fine etcher over the surface, and the untorn shells lie thick upon the sand, and the tops of the rocks, to which the waves never rise, are green with grass grown fine as hair. It is the landscape, not of dreams or fancy, but of places far withdrawn, and hours selected from a thousand with a miracle of finesse. Through his strange

veil of sight things reach him so; in no ordinary
night or day, but as in faint light of eclipse, or in
some brief interval of falling rain at daybreak, or
through deep water.

And not into nature only; but he plunged also
into human personality, and became above all a
painter of portraits; faces of a modelling more
skilful than has been seen before or since, embodied
with a reality which almost amounts to illusion
on dark air. To take a character as it was, and
delicately sound its stops, suited one so curious
in observation, curious in invention. So he painted
the portraits of Ludovico's mistresses, Lucretia
Crivelli and Cecilia Galerani the poetess, of Ludovico himself, and the Duchess Beatrice. The
portrait of Cecilia Galerani is lost, but that of
Lucretia Crivelli has been identified with La
Belle Ferronnière of the Louvre, and Ludovico's
pale, anxious face still remains in the Ambrosian.
Opposite is the portrait of Beatrice d'Este, in whom
Leonardo seems to have caught some presentiment
of early death, painting her precise and grave, full
of the refinement of the dead, in sad earth-coloured
raiment, set with pale stones.

Sometimes this curiosity came in conflict with
the desire of beauty; it tended to make him go
too far below that outside of things in which art
begins and ends. This struggle between the reason
and its ideas and the senses, the desire of beauty,
is the key to Leonardo's life at Milan—his restlessness, his endless retouchings, his odd experiments

with colour. How much must he leave unfinished, how much recommence! His problem was the transmutation of ideas into images. What he had attained so far had been the mastery of that earlier Florentine style, with its naïve and limited sensuousness. Now he was to entertain in this narrow medium those divinations of a humanity too wide for it—that larger vision of the opening world which is only not too much for the great irregular art of Shakespeare; and everywhere the effort is visible in the work of his hands. This agitation, this perpetual delay, give him an air of weariness and ennui. To others he seems to be aiming at an impossible effect, to do something that art, that painting, can never do. Often the expression of physical beauty at this or that point seems strained and marred in the effort, as in those heavy German foreheads—too heavy and German for perfect beauty.

There was a touch of Germany in that genius which, as Goethe said, had " müde sich gedacht," *thought itself weary.* What an anticipation of modern Germany, for instance, in that debate on the question whether sculpture or painting is the nobler art! [1] But there is this difference between him and the German, that, with all that curious science, the German would have thought nothing more was needed; and the name of Goethe himself

[1] How princely, how characteristic of Leonardo, the answer, "Quanto piu', un' arte porta seco fatica di corpo, tanto più è vile"!

reminds one how great for the artist may be the danger of over-much science; how Goethe, who, in the *Elective Affinities* and the first part of *Faust*, does transmute ideas into images, who wrought many such transmutations, did not invariably find the spell-word, and in the second part of *Faust*, presents us with a mass of science which has no artistic character at all. But Leonardo will never work till the happy moment comes—that moment of *bien-être*, which to imaginative men is a moment of invention. On this moment he waits; other moments are but a preparation or after-taste of it. Few men distinguish between them as jealously as he did. Hence so many flaws even in the choicest work. But for Leonardo the distinction is absolute, and in the moment of *bien-être* the alchemy complete; the idea is stricken into colour and imagery; a cloudy mysticism is refined to a subdued and graceful mystery, and painting pleases the eye while it satisfies the soul.

This curious beauty is seen above all in his drawings, and in these chiefly in the abstract grace of the bounding lines. Let us take some of these drawings, and pause over them awhile; and, first, one of those at Florence—the heads of a woman and a little child, set side by side, but each in its own separate frame. First of all, there is something exquisitely tender in the re-appearance in the fuller curves of the child, of the sharper, more chastened lines of the worn and older face, which leaves no doubt that the heads are those of a little child and its mother, indicative of a feeling for maternity always characteristic of Leonardo; a feeling further indicated here by the half-humorous pathos of the diminutive rounded shoulders of the child. You may note a like tenderness in drawings of a young man, seated in a stooping posture, his face in his hands, as in sorrow; of a slave sitting in an uneasy sitting attitude in some brief interval of rest; of a small Madonna and Child, peeping sideways in half-reassured terror, as a mighty griffin with bat-like wings—one of Leonardo's finest *inventions*, —descends suddenly from the air to snatch up a lion wandering near them. But note in these, as that which especially belongs to art, the contour of the young man's hair, the poise of the slave's arm above his head, and the curves of the head of the child, following the little skull within, thin and fine as some sea-shell worn by the wind.

Take again another head, still more full of sentiment, but of a different kind—a little red chalk drawing which every one remembers who has seen the drawings at the Louvre. It is a face of doubtful sex, set in the shadow of its own hair, the cheek-line in high light against it, with something voluptuous and full in the eyelids and the lips. Another drawing might pass for the same face in childhood, with parched and feverish lips, but with much sweetness in the loose, short-waisted, childish dress, with necklace and *bulla*, and the daintily bound hair. We might take the thread of

suggestion which these two drawings offer, thus
set side by side, and, following it through the
drawings at Florence, Venice, and Milan, con-
struct a sort of series, illustrating better than anything else Leonardo's type of womanly beauty.
Daughters of Herodias, their fantastic head-dresses
knotted and folded so strangely, to leave the dainty
oval of the face disengaged, they are not of the
Christian family, or of Raffaelle's. They are the
clairvoyants, through whom, as through delicate
instruments, one becomes aware of the subtler
forces of nature, and the modes of their action, all
that is magnetic in it, all those finer conditions
wherein material things rise to that subtlety of
operation which constitutes them spiritual, where
only the finer nerve and the keener touch can
follow; it is as if in certain revealing instances
we actually saw them at their work on human
flesh. Nervous, electric, faint always with some
inexplicable faintness, they seem to be subject to
exceptional conditions, to feel powers at work in
the common air unfelt by others, to become, as
it were, receptacles of them, and pass them on to
us in a chain of secret influences.

But among the more youthful heads there is one
at Florence which Love chooses for its own—the
head of a young man, which may well be the likeness of Salaino, beloved of Leonardo for his curled
and waving hair—*belli capelli ricci e inanellati*—
and afterwards his favourite pupil and servant. Of
all the interests in living men and women which

may have filled his life at Milan, this attachment
alone is recorded; and in return, Salaino identified
himself so entirely with Leonardo, that the picture
of St. Anne, in the Louvre, has been attributed
to him. It illustrates Leonardo's usual choice of
pupils—men of some natural charm of person or
intercourse, like Salaino; or men of birth and
princely habits of life, like Francesco Melzi—men
with just enough genius to be capable of initiation
into his secret, for which they were ready to efface
their own individuality. Among them, retiring
often to the villa of the Melzi at Canonica al
Vaprio, he worked at his fugitive manuscripts
and sketches, working for the present hour, and
for a few only, perhaps chiefly for himself. Other
artists have been as careless of present or future
applause, in self-forgetfulness, or because they set
moral or political ends above the ends of art; but
in him this solitary culture of beauty seems to have
hung upon a kind of self-love, and a carelessness
in the work of art of all but art itself. Out of the
secret places of a unique temperament he brought
strange blossoms and fruits hitherto unknown;
and for him the novel impression conveyed, the
exquisite effect woven, counted as an end in itself
—a perfect end.

And these pupils of his acquired his manner so
thoroughly, that though the number of Leonardo's
authentic works is very small indeed, there is a
multitude of other men's pictures, through which
we undoubtedly see him and come very near to

LEONARDO DA VINCI

his genius. Sometimes, as in the little picture of
the Madonna of the Balances, in which, from the
bosom of his mother, Christ weighs the pebbles of
the brook against the sins of men, we have a hand,
rough enough by contrast, working on some fine
hint or sketch of his. Sometimes, as in the subjects
of the daughter of Herodias and the head of John
the Baptist, the lost originals have been re-echoed
and varied upon again and again by Luini and
others. At other times the original remains, but
has been a mere theme or motive, a type of which
the accessories might be modified or changed;
and these variations have but brought out the
more the purpose or expression of the original.
It is so with the so-called St. John the Baptist of
the Louvre—one of the few naked figures Leonardo
painted—whose delicate brown flesh and woman's
hair no one would go out into the wilderness to
seek, and whose treacherous smile would have
us understand something far beyond the outward
gesture or circumstance. But the long reed-like
cross in the hand, which suggests John the Baptist,
becomes faint in a copy at the Ambrosian, and
disappears altogether in another in the Palazzo
Rosso at Genoa. Returning from the last to the
original, we are no longer surprised by St. John's
strange likeness to the Bacchus, which hangs near
it, which set Gautier thinking of Heine's notion
of decayed gods, who, to maintain themselves,
took employment in the new religion. We recognise
one of those symbolical inventions in which the

179

ostensible subject is used, not as matter for definite pictorial realisation, but as the starting-point of a train of sentiment, subtle and vague as a piece of music. No one ever ruled over his subject more entirely than Leonardo, or bent it more dexterously to purely artistic ends. And so it comes to pass that though he handles sacred subjects continually, he is the most profane of painters; the given person or subject, Saint John in the Desert, or the Virgin on the Knees of Saint Anne, is often merely the pretext for a kind of work which carries one quite out of the range of its conventional associations.

About the Last Supper, its decay and restorations, a whole literature has risen up, Goethe's pensive sketch of its sad fortunes being far the best. The death in child-birth of the Duchess Beatrice, was followed in Ludovico by one of those paroxysms of religious feeling which in him were constitutional. The low gloomy, Dominican church of Saint Mary of the Graces had been the favourite shrine of Beatrice. She had spent her last days there, full of sinister presentiments; at last it had been almost necessary to remove her from it by force. And now it was here that mass was said a hundred times a day for her repose; and a mania for restoring churches took possession of the duke. So on the damp wall of the refectory, oozing with mineral salts, Leonardo painted the Last Supper. A hundred anecdotes were told about it, his retouchings and delays. They show him refusing to work except at the moment of invention, scornful of whoever thought that art was a work of mere industry and rule, often coming the whole length of Milan to give a single touch. He painted it, not in fresco, where all must be *impromptu*, but in oils, the new method which he had been one of the first to welcome, because it allowed of so many after-thoughts, such a refined working out of perfection. It turned out that on a plastered wall no process could have been less durable. Within fifty years it had fallen into decay. Protestants, who always found themselves much edified by a certain biblical turn in it, have multiplied all sorts of bad copies and engravings of it. And now we have to turn back to Leonardo's own studies,— above all, to one drawing of the central head at the Brera, which in a union of tenderness and severity in the face-lines, reminds one of the monumental work of Mino da Fiesole,—to trace it as it was.

It was another effort to set a thing out of the range of its conventional associations. Strange, after all the misrepresentations of the Middle Age, was the effort to see it, not as the pale host of the altar, but as one taking leave of his friends. Five years after, the young Raffaelle, at Florence, painted it with sweet and solemn effect in the refectory of Saint Onofrio; but still with all the mystical unreality of the school of Perugino. Vasari pretends that the central head was never finished. Well; finished or unfinished, or owing part of its effect to a mellowing decay, this central head does but consummate the sentiment of the whole company—ghosts through which you see the wall, faint as the shadows of the leaves upon the wall on autumn afternoons; this figure is but the faintest, most spectral of them all. It is the image of what the history it symbolises has been more and more ever since, paler and paler as it recedes from us. Criticism came with its appeal from mystical unrealities to originals, and restored no life-like reality but these transparent shadows — spirits which have not flesh and bones.

The Last Supper was finished in 1497; in 1498 the French entered Milan, and whether or not the Gascon bowmen used it as a mark for their arrows,[1] the model of the Sforza certainly did not survive. Ludovico became a prisoner, and the remaining years of Leonardo's life are more or less years of wandering. From his brilliant life at court he had saved nothing, and he returned to Florence a poor man. Perhaps necessity kept his spirit excited: the next four years are one prolonged rapture or ecstasy of invention. He painted the pictures of the Louvre, his most authentic works, which came there straight from the cabinet of Francis I. at Fontainebleau. One picture of his, the Saint Anne—not the Saint Anne of the Louvre, but a mere cartoon now in London

[1] M. Arsène Houssaye comes to save the credit of his countrymen.

—revived for a moment a sort of appreciation more
common in an earlier time, when good pictures
had still seemed miraculous; and for two days a
crowd of people of all qualities passed in naïve
excitement through the chamber where it hung,
and gave him a taste of Cimabue's triumph. But
his work was less with the saints than with the
living women of Florence; for he moved still in
the polished society that he loved, and in the salons
of Florence, left perhaps a little subject to light
thoughts by the death of Savonarola (the latest
gossip is of an undraped Monna Lisa, found in
some out-of-the-way corner of the late Orleans
collection), he met Ginevra di Benci, and Lisa,
the young third wife of Francesco del Giocondo.
As we have seen him using incidents of the sacred
legend, not for their own sake, or as mere subjects
for pictorial realisation, but as a symbolical language for fancies all his own, so now he found a
vent for his thoughts in taking one of these languid
women, and raising her, as Leda or Pomona,
Modesty or Vanity, to the seventh heaven of
symbolical expression.

La Gioconda is, in the truest sense, Leonardo's masterpiece—the revealing instance of his
mode of thought and work. In suggestiveness,
only the Melancholia of Dürer is comparable
to it; and no crude symbolism disturbs the effect
of its subdued and graceful mystery. We all know
the face and hands of the figure, set in its marble
chair, in that cirque of fantastic rocks, as in some

faint light under sea. Perhaps of all ancient pictures time has chilled it least.[1] As often happens with works in which invention seems to reach its limit, there is an element in it given to, not invented by, the master. In that inestimable folio of drawings, once in the possession of Vasari, were certain designs by Verrocchio—faces of such impressive beauty that Leonardo in his boyhood copied them many times. It is hard not to connect with these designs of the elder by-past master, as with its germinal principle, the unfathomable smile, always with a touch of something sinister in it, which plays over all Leonardo's work. Besides the picture is a portrait. From childhood we see this image defining itself on the fabric of his dreams; and but for express historical testimony, we might fancy that this was but his ideal lady, embodied and beheld at last. What was the relationship of a living Florentine to this creature of his thought? By what strange affinities had she and the dream grown thus apart, yet so closely together? Present from the first incorporeal in Leonardo's thought, dimly traced in the designs of Verrochio, she is found present at last in Il Giocondo's house. That there is much of mere portraiture in the picture is attested by the legend that by artificial means, the presence of mimes and flute-players, that subtle expression was protracted on the face. Again, was it in four years and by renewed labour never really completed,

---

[1] Yet for Vasari there was some further magic of crimson in the lips and cheeks, lost for us.

or in four months, and as by stroke of magic, that
the image was projected?

The presence that thus so strangely rose beside
the waters is expressive of what in the ways of a
thousand years man had come to desire. Hers is
the head upon which all " the ends of the world
are come," and the eyelids are a little weary. It
is a beauty wrought out from within upon the
flesh—the deposit, little cell by cell, of strange
thoughts and fantastic reveries and exquisite passions.
Set it for a moment beside one of those white Greek
goddesses or beautiful women of antiquity, and
how would they be troubled by this beauty, into
which the soul with all its maladies has passed?
All the thoughts and experiences of the world
have etched and moulded therein that which they
have of power to refine and make expressive the
outward form—the animalism of Greece, the lust
of Rome, the reverie of the Middle Age with its
spiritual ambition and imaginative loves, the return
of the Pagan world, the sins of the Borgias. She
is older than the rocks among which she sits; like
the vampire, she has been dead many times, and
learned the secrets of the grave; and has been a
diver in deep seas, and keeps their fallen day about
her; and trafficked for strange webs with Eastern
merchants; and, as Leda, was the mother of Helen
of Troy, and, as Saint Anne, the mother of Mary;
and all this has been to her but as the sound of lyres
and flutes, and lives only in the delicacy with which
it has moulded the changing lineaments and tinged

the eyelids and the hands. The fancy of a perpetual life, sweeping together ten thousand experiences, is an old one; and modern thought has conceived the idea of humanity as wrought upon by, and summing up in itself, all modes of thought and life. Certainly, Lady Lisa might stand as the embodiment of the old fancy, the symbol of the modern idea.

During these years at Florence Leonardo's history is the history of his art; he himself is lost in the bright cloud of it. The outward history begins again in 1502, with a wild journey through central Italy, which he makes as the chief engineer of Cæsar Borgia. The biographer, putting together the stray jottings of his MSS., may follow him through every day of it, up the strange tower of Sienna, which looks towards Rome, elastic like a bent bow, down to the seashore at Piombino, each place appearing as fitfully as in a fever dream.

One other great work was left for him to do— a work all trace of which soon vanished—the Battle of the Standard, in which he had for his rival Michael Angelo. The citizens of Florence, desiring to decorate the walls of the great council chambers, had offered the work for competition, and any subject might be chosen from the Florentine wars of the fifteenth century. Michael Angelo chose for his cartoon an incident of the war with Pisa, in which the Florentine soldiers, bathing in the Arno, are surprised by the sound of trumpets, and run to arms. His design has reached us only in an old engraving, which perhaps would help

us less than what we remember of the background
of his Holy Family in the Uffizi to imagine
in what superhuman form, such as might have
beguiled the heart of an earlier world, those figures
may have risen from the water. Leonardo chose
an incident from the battle of Anghiari, in which
two parties of soldiers fight for a standard. Like
Michael Angelo's, his cartoon is lost, and has come
to us only in sketches and a fragment of Rubens.
Through the accounts given we may discern some
lust of terrible things in it, so that even the horses
tore each other with their teeth; and yet one
fragment of it, in a drawing of his at Florence, is
far different—a waving field of lovely armour, the
chased edgings running like lines of sunlight from
side to side. Michael Angelo was twenty-seven
years old; Leonardo more than fifty; and Raffaelle,
then nineteen years old, visiting Florence for the
first time, came and watched them as they worked.

We catch a glimpse of him again at Rome in
1514, surrounded by his mirrors and vials and
furnaces, making strange toys that seemed alive of
wax and quicksilver. The hesitation which had
haunted him all through life, and made him like
one under a spell, was on him now with double
force. No one had ever carried political indifferentism farther; it had always been his philosophy
to " fly before the storm "; he is out with the
Sforzas and in with the Sforzas as the tide of fortune
turns. Yet now he was suspected by the anti-
Gallican, Medicean society at Rome, of French

leanings. It paralysed him to find himself among enemies; and he turned wholly to France, which had long courted him.

France was going to be an Italy more Italian than Italy itself. Francis I., like Louis XII. before him, was attracted by the finesse of Leonardo's work. La Gioconda was already in his cabinet, and he offered Leonardo the little Château de Clou, with its vineyards and meadows, in the soft valley of the Masse—not too far from the great outer sea. M. Arsène Houssaye has succeeded in giving a pensive local colour to this part of his subject, with which, as a Frenchman, he could best deal. "A Monsieur Lyonard, peintre du Roy pour Amboyse," so the letter of Francis I. is headed. It opens a prospect—one of the most attractive in the history of art—where, under a strange mixture of lights, Italian art dies away as a French exotic. M. Houssaye does but touch it lightly, and it would carry us beyond the present essay if we allowed ourselves to be seduced by its interest.

Two questions remain, after all busy antiquarianism, concerning Leonardo's death—the question of his religion, and the question whether Francis I. was present at the time. They are of about equally little importance in the estimate of Leonardo's genius. The directions in his will about the thirty masses and the great candles for the church of St. Florentin are things of course—their real purpose being immediate and practical; and on no theory of religion could such hurried candle-burning be of much consequence. We forget them in speculating how one who had been always so desirous of beauty, but desired it always in such precise and definite forms, as hands or flowers or hair, looked forward now into the vague land, and experienced the last curiosity.

THE ROMANCE OF THE PEERAGE

By Frederic Harrison

Nôsse omnia hæc salus *esset senioribus.*

The rest of his dress—a dress always sufficiently tawdry—was overcharged with lace, embroidery, and ornament of every kind; and the plume of feathers which he wore was so high, as if intended to sweep the roof of the hall. In short, the usual gaudy splendour of the heraldic attire was caricatured and overdone.

> (*See Walter Scott's "Quentin Durward"—Hayraddin, the Gipsy, goes to the Court of Charles the Bold, disguised as Rouge Sanglier, the herald.*)

ON the eve of the great Revolution in France, when society was in its most rickety, but not its most corrupt stage, a man of genius painted it to the life in a very diverting play. It was one of the most curious features of that unconscious age, that it delighted in pleasant caricatures of itself. As Carlyle tells us in the opening of his history, " Beaumarchais (or De Beaumarchais, for he got ennobled) had been born poor, but aspiring, esurient; with talents, audacity, adroitness; above all, with a talent for intrigue; a lean, but also a tough indomitable man." The theme of his plays was

Fashion, his hero a valet; and being a sort of inspired valet, or *factotum*, himself, he hit off with art the great world as seen from the valet point of view. Figaro, the adventurer, the factotum, the prince of rascals, became quite the rage; and the delicious impudence which he threw into his servility, exactly caught the public ear. Men laughed to see the fatuous pomp of the *ancien régime* treated with a kind of fawning mockery by one of its own creatures. But the loudest laughter came from the great people, in whose faces the witty Barber was snapping his fingers.

In the midst of it all the Revolution burst, and swept away play and player, stage, company, scenery, dresses, and all the gorgeous accessories; and our poor friend saw his comedy end in a very grim catastrophe—which he had done not a little to hasten.

History, for all that they say, does not reproduce itself. In the first place, we have no Revolution, nor indeed, with our admirable constitution, are we likely to have. And most certainly we have no Beaumarchais. The humour and the grace of the delightful Sevillard are as much a thing of the past as the *ancienne noblesse*. Still we have, even in our day, a society luxurious and absurd enough, although sadly turned into prose. And we have a man of wit who has studied it from life—one-half Jester, one-half Grand Master of the Ceremonies.

Lothair is not a mere novel; and its appearance is not simply a fact for Mr. Mudie. It is a political event. When a man whose life has been passed in Parliament, who for a generation has been the real head of a great party, sits down, as he approaches the age of seventy, to embody his view of modern life, it is a matter of interest to the politician, the historian, nay, almost the philosopher. The literary qualities of the book need detain no man. Premiers not uncommonly do write sad stuff. And we should be thankful if the stuff only be amusing. But the mature thoughts on life of one who has governed an empire on which the sun never sets, have an inner meaning to the thoughtful mind. Marcus Aurelius, amidst his imperial eagles, thought right to give us his Reflections. The sayings of Napoleon at St. Helena have a strange interest to all men. And Solomon in all his glory was induced to publish some amazing rhapsodies on human nature and the society of his own time.

Lothair is indeed amusing. Though our grave Editor warns us that these pages are more fitted for what he calls " the social and political significance " of the book, we cannot resist one word of admiration for the brilliance, and indeed rare wit, of much in the writing. There are epigrams in showers, some of them really delicious. That phrase about the critics is perfect, and as true as it is amusing. The Duke who, as he gives the finishing touch to his consummate toilette, each day thanks Providence that his family are not unworthy of him; St. Aldegonde, a Duke's son and a Duke's son-in-law, proposing to abolish all orders of men

but Dukes, and calling for cold meat at Lord—
we mean Mr.—Brancepeth's dinner-party; the
professor who during a stroll gives more than one
receipt for saving the aristocracy; the comparing
our young nobles to the ancient Greeks, who were
good athletes, knew no language but their own,
and never read; the Hansom cab, "the gondola
of London," are the touches of a master. For our
author, when not in court dress, is before everything a wit.

Then the dialogue is quick, bright, and easy.
The scenes follow with vivacious variety. St.
Aldegonde himself might read it without being
bored. Nothing lingers. Our author receives his
ideal company like an accomplished host. A word
for this one; a happy saying to that; a skilful
selection of guests; the mind diverted now with
this, now with that, entertainment. The characters
even have merit. Not that they are characters in
the creative sense, but they are happy satirettes.
The fatuous Duke, the goose Lothair, the spiritual
Cardinal, are portraits not perhaps of true humour,
but of a caustic, albeit rather personal, wit. And
all this, which is so rare in an English book, is
exceedingly pleasant to find. The wit, the light
touch, the movement, are those of an accomplished
foreigner—a sort of Mr. Pinto surveying British
society from without, and trying to amuse it. The
colouring often rises to a high point of art; and
society is analysed with something of almost poetic
instinct. Not that we wish to exaggerate. We do

not pretend that the art is that of Balzac or Sand,
or the wit that of the true children of Voltaire.
But it is quite as good as that of a first-rate Parisian
feuilleton—and there are few things better.

Nor must one omit another great merit. *Lothair*
is clean. Not only is it free from offence in language,
but the tone in point of morals is healthy, pure,
and sweet. The society painted is, on the whole,
that of honest husbands and true wives, pure maidens
and ingenuous lads. This is a great point. We hear
nothing of those *petit crevé* vices, those pornerastic
habits in high places, those Diamond-necklace
scandals, those unmentionable gambols of the
Porphyro-geniti, which are too often thrust before
our eyes in fiction, and indeed in fact. Society owes
much to Mr. Disraeli for this. If he is to be believed,
it is a society of real happy and healthy homes; and
he speaks of them almost as one inspired by some
influence that had been the good genius and true
pride of his life.

Not that we are blind in our praise of this book.
The writing, though often brilliant, is curiously
loose and false. To speak the truth, there is hardly
a page without clumsy phrases, misused words,
and even hopelessly bad grammar. Nor is this the
worst. Not only do gross solecisms, but absolute
cockneyisms abound; the high-polite jargon and
the genteel vulgarisms of a hairdresser's man. We
do not for a moment attribute this to Mr. Disraeli
himself, a master alike of the language of letters
and of society; and we believe we are in a position

to explain, as we presently shall, this curious phenomenon. But strange as it may sound, the fact
remains. And the style of the ex-Premier's romance
reminds one not seldom of the style in which
ambitious lady's-maids and literary valets write
romances for the *Mirror of Fashion* (a publication
read in the highest circles).

We think some bits must have been written for
and refused by the *Mirror*. For instance, a young
lady of rank (of course everybody in the book is
of the highest rank; the readers of the *Mirror*
expect nothing below earls)—a young lady talks
to the hero about their "*mutual ancestors.*" Shade
of Macaulay! One used to think that *mutual* friend
for *common* friend was rather a cockneyism. But
mutual ancestors! Oh, right honourable sir! *mutual,*
as Johnson will tell us, means something reciprocal,
a giving and taking. How could people have mutual
ancestors ? — unless, indeed, their great grand-
parents had exchanged husbands or wives—a
horrid thought!

Then we hear of a "gay and festive and *cordial*
scene." A festive scene we can understand, and a
cordial host. But what is a "cordial" scene ?
The late Artemus Ward used to speak of "a gay
and festive cuss." But a "gay and festive and
cordial scene" would beat the showman!

A gentleman (by the way, almost the only
commoner in society—but then he is after all but
the family solicitor, a superior sort of "retainer"),
a gentleman is spoken of who "had, in her circles,

a celebrated wife." How can a man have a wife
in her circles ? Does it mean a lady of ample skirts
and hoops, or of ample and globular form ? Again,
we hear that " All the ladies of the house were
fond and fine horsewomen." Fine women, we can
understand, and fine horsewomen, but what is a
fond horsewoman ? Of what are these ladies fond ?
Mr. Pinto tells us that the English language consists of only four words, " to which some gram-
marians add fond." We are afraid that Mr. Pinto,
though almost naturalised amongst us, has not yet
mastered the varieties of the English tongue.

Riding parties linger *amid* a breeze. A lady
makes observations cheapening *to* her host, meaning
depreciating her host, not, we trust, that she made
them to her host. " Bells of prancing ponies,
lashed by delicate hands, *gingle* in the laughing air."
We think the poor whipping-boy, the printer,
must have been laughing too when he set up *gingle*.
" Obstructive dependants *impede the convenience*
they were purposed to facilitate." A trustee
" guards *over* an inheritance." Some one considers,
" where he shall go *to*." Two great ladies " are
the fairies, *which* do " something. The hero holds
" his groom's horse, who had dismounted." Who
dismounted ? Did the groom dismount off the
horse, or the horse off the groom ? Heroes may do
feats, but can their grooms ? A lady's portrait
" makes a fury." Of two lovers it is said, " Then,
clinging to him, he induced her to resume her
stroll." Who was clinging to whom ? Each, doubt-

less, to each " *mutually* "; but it is horribly suggestive of a third person, and that person a male.

Oh! Editor of the *Mirror of Fashion*, lucky, *tua si bona nôris*, wert thou in a contributor who had carried the high-polite Euphuism to a point yet unattained in thy peculiar industry. Let us cull some flowers from the garden of the Lady Corisande!

Of a riding party—" Dames and damsels vault on their barbs and genets with airy majesty." Airy majesty is good!

A gentleman bows—" He made a reverence of ceremony." Couldst thou do that, Yellowplush?

One college lad goes to see another—" He becomes a visitor to his domain."

Some servants waiting in a hall—" Half a dozen powdered gentlemen, glowing in crimson liveries, indicate the presence of My Lord's footmen." Prodigious! as Dominie Sampson used to say.

Charity boys are brought out with their school flags to meet the squire—" Choirs of enthusiastic children, waving parochial banners, hymned his auspicious approach."

A man gives a girl some lemonade and a wafer, and tells her she is looking in good spirits—" He fed her with cates, as delicate as her lips, and manufactured for her dainty beverages which would not outrage their purity, and at last could not refrain from intimating his sense of her unusual, but charming joyousness." (See the Vade-mecum of Etiquette.)

Fine rooms are "stately" or "choice saloons."
Footmen are "retainers." Men of rank are
"paladins of high degree." Cut glass is "fanciful
crystal." A dinner-party is a "banquet." A gun-
club are "competing confederates." A ball is a
"sumptuous festival"; the guests are "wassailers."
A carriage is always an "equipage"; and a horse
always a "barb."

All this points to an origin rather to be sought
in the species of male serving-man, or as one should
say, "indicates the presence of My Lord's footmen"; but there are traces again which point to
a female coadjutor, as of some lady's-maid, with
whom said lackey was in love. For instance, a
croquet-party "makes up a sparkling and *modish*
scene." "Modish" is surely a little out of date,
and savours of the housekeeper's room. Of a ball-
room supper we hear, "Never was such an elegant
clatter." A young lady "is the cynosure of the
Empyrean." A youth courting her, "seals, with
an embrace, her speechless form." To seal, it is
true, in Mormon-land is to marry. When the
young lady goes to Court, "Her fair cheek is
sealed with the approbation of Majesty"—*sealed*
again. When a man speaks of the Court, "He
leads the conversation to the majestic theme."
Stars and Garters!

Have a care, good Editor, and tone down their
style! They are fooling thee with their menial
jargon. Be warned, friend, educated Englishmen
do not write like this:

" When the stranger who had proved so oppor-
tune an ally to Lothair at the Fenian meeting,
separated from his companion, he proceeded in
the direction of Pentonville, and, after pursuing
his way through a number of obscure streets, *but*
quiet, decent, and monotonous, he stopped at a
small house in a row of many *residences, yet* all of
them in form, size, colour, and general character
so identical, that the number on the door could
alone assure the visitor that he was not in error
when he *sounded the knocker*."

What is all this jumble of words, with its draggled
sentences, and " buts," and " thats," and " yets."
" *So* identical!" " So similar " you mean. " So
identical " is lady's-maid's English; and why
" obscure streets, *but* quiet, decent, etc." ? Can
nothing obscure be decent ? Why not write like
a man, and say—" When the stranger who had
helped Lothair at the Fenian meeting *left* his companion, he *walked towards* Pentonville, making
his way through several obscure streets, *which were*
quiet, decent, and monotonous. He stopped at a
small house in a long row, where the *houses* were
so similar in form, size, colour, and general character,
that, but for the number, one might easily *knock
at the wrong door*."

But as for grand ceremonies, O Editor! thy
contributor out-herods Herod, and beggars all
previous description of *haut ton*. The *Court News-
man* grows pale with envy; Jenkyns of the *Morning
Plush* is awed. Thy hebdomadal competitors do

reverence to their peerless rival. Ho! there, a
flourish! Bray forth trumpets, and heralds advance
your haughty blazonry! Make way, ye fellows in
fustian! Stand back, I charge ye!

[*A march!*

" Royalty, followed by the imperial presence of
ambassadors, and escorted by a group of
dazzling duchesses and paladins of high degree,
was ushered with courteous pomp by the host
and hostess into a choice saloon, hung with
rose-coloured tapestry and illumined by chan-
deliers of crystal, where they were served
from gold plate."

[*Curtain falls, amidst catharine wheels, red
and blue fire, electric light, etc., etc., etc.*

Shade of the late George Robins of the Hammer,
greatest of auctioneers, here is a greater than thou
in unctuous description of all kinds of upholstery!
Greatest of all Editors of Trans-atlantic news-
papers, here is taller talk than in the wildest of thy
dreams, which is to thy best vein as is thy own
Niagara to a gutter, or thy *Wellingtonia gigantea*
to a gooseberry bush! O tallest of talkers! canst
thou match " buncombe " like that? O most
superb of auctioneers, didst thou ever appraise
and bring to the hammer (without any reserve)
the entire British Aristocracy, rose-coloured tapestry, gold plate, and all—nay, the Majestic Theme
itself, it would seem—as Lot 1?

As we have said, we do not for a moment pretend

that jargon of this kind really comes from Mr. Disraeli. He is a man of genius, a master of language, and has passed his life in refined society. He is incapable of inditing this stuff. Of course, all sorts of rumours are afloat; but we rather gather the truth to be this: Mr. Disraeli, a busy statesman, employed assistance; that assistance he would naturally find in his " people " in attendance. The ideas, the wit, the picture of society are his own, but we strongly suspect that the actual wording not seldom is that of his valet.

What we imagine to have taken place—we speak with no authority—is something of this kind: The great orator returns, say, from a debate in which he has exterminated the Liberal party for the twenty-seventh time, and given new hope to his country and his Sovereign. He has an hour of relaxation. Robed, doubtless, in some cashmere dressing-gown which had once graced the throne of the Great Mogul, shod with the jewelled slippers that had haply been worked for him by the daughter of the Emperor of Morocco (an unhappy attachment, it is whispered), and smoking his hookah, with its bowl of solid topaz, and its mouthpiece a single diamond (a trifle from the Sublime Porte), the wondrous orator throws off the dazzling fancies of *Lothair*. Thoughts crowd so fast on that fervid soul, that three stenographers can but imperfectly record them as he speaks. And the valet, or one should say, the first gentleman of the dressing-room, takes forth the burning fragments on golden salvers to cast them into readable volumes for Messrs. Longman, who are waiting in an ante-room. Thus it is that we get the ideas of a true wit and the experience of a profound observer in the language of the servants' hall, and her ladyship's first gentlewoman.

Now without intruding on private affairs— the frank Lothair is free from modesty of that kind—we strongly suspect this first gentleman of the dressing-room to be a person of foreign birth. We know not how else to account for the use of crude Gallicisms, such as no Englishman could pen. A perplexing use of the word "but"; a lady's portrait "making a fury"; things "being on the carpet"; and a reckless use of the word "distinguished" for fine; phrases like "an alliance of the highest," "high ceremony of manner," "his affairs were great" for his trade, betray the foreign hand. We have no doubt this great creature, the first gentleman in question, is a perfect treasure. But if he continue to be employed as secretary, the ex-Premier should present him with Lindley Murray—of course bound in jewelled vellum, with gilt edges.

But the misplaced confidence which the right honourable gentleman appears to have reposed in his "first gentleman," has led to some more serious errors in taste. We make nothing of a few slips. "*Lancres*" is not the right mode of spelling the painter's name, nor is "*monsignores*" a correct form. And the Pope's guard is the *guardia* (not *guarda) nobile.* Perhaps these little blunders in foreign languages are a compliment to the order " which knows no language but its own." We do not like to hear of " costly bindings " in a library. There was an honest man once who cared more for the inside of books than their " costly " backs. But in the midst of the praises which we wish to give to this amusing romance of real life, there is one serious fault which we condemn.

It seems to us that, elegant as the company are, they are painted as if the real object of their respect, their social standard in fact, were, in plain words, Money. Every one in the book is enormously rich, and no one beside appears to count as a member of society at all. The society is a mere Apotheosis of rich men—the Reign of the Financial Saints—a perfect *Millionairium*; One would think the author were Poet-Laureate to Baron Rothschild. The very attorney is a Six-and-eightpenny Sidonia!

Nowhere perhaps is this so marked as when the Duke himself tells us that he has known Americans who were very good sort of people, and had no end of money (*sic*); that he looks upon one who has large estates in the South as a real aristocrat, and should always treat him with respect—more especially if, like the colonel, his territory is immense, and he has always lived in the highest style (*sic*). This may be satire, or it may be fact, but we venture to think it both gross and untrue. Peers may sometimes be foolish, and possibly proud;

but they are usually English gentlemen, and we doubt if they talk with the purse-proud insolence of Tittlebat Titmouse. But a man who has made Dukes ought to know best.

But all this time we are sadly forgetting what our grave Editor calls the "social and political significance" of *Lothair*, and are thinking too much of the many merits and occasional slips of its literary work. As a novel it may be called good, and that is the principal point. The story, if improbable and rambling, is tolerably amusing and not outrageously absurd. The characters, though not creations, are keen sketches of social types. And the raving about Semitism, Popery, and the Brotherhoods is but a tithe of what one endured in *Tancred* and the *Wondrous Tale*. Indeed, one has heard wilder stuff from the author's lips in grave political speeches at times of excitement. Even the bombast hardly equals that immortal bit about "the elephants of Asia carrying the artillery of Europe over the mountains of Africa through passes which might appal the trapper of the Rocky Mountains." Nor do we compare the plot for sensational power with those of that gorgeous Titan Eugene Sue; nor the *mise-en-scène* for profusion with that of the inexhaustible wizard of *Monte Cristo*. Still, the novel, as novels go, is a good one.

But as to the substance of the book, for the Editor grows impatient, it is strange how much opinions differ. There are not wanting some who speak harshly—the men no doubt "who have failed." We believe them to be really unjust. But their reasons are worth considering. "How gross it is," said to us a serious friend of advanced views, a Republican, when we asked his opinion of "the novel." "If snobbishness be," he went on, "as Thackeray defines it, the mean admiration of mean things, was ever book so unutterably snobbish? Was ever the fatuous pomp of grandees, the accident not even of ancient traditions, but of mere conventional rank; were ever the coarsest show of money and what money can buy, the selfish vagaries of a besotted caste, more stupidly and fawningly belauded? Where find such noisy grovelling before wealth and state? Is not a taste for liveried footmen in themselves, and costly bindings in themselves, essentially a mean taste? Is not the truckling to a rich idiotic boy, and the wanton fooleries of idle wealth, a mean thing? Can these mean things be more meanly admired than in a book every line of which is rank with fulsome grandiloquence?"

"Bah, friend," said we to the serious man, "you take all this in your fierce way, *au grand sérieux.* The object of a novel is to amuse. The artist passes no judgments; his business is to paint persons and scenes. Here we have a picture of a state of society, more or less true to life; there is much that is very diverting, and presents us with human nature. The public likes to hear of the great. No doubt you were interested yourself."

"No," said our serious friend, almost bitterly,

and wholly unconscious of our little rap; "I do not judge the book by the standard of the trash in green covers, or of the boyish freaks of a Vivian Gray. It comes from one who has led the governing classes, and ruled this country for years, at the close of a long political career 'Noblesse oblige,' they say. 'Esprit oblige,' I say. And if this be the picture of that order, which a man of genius, who has made it his tool, can sit down in his old age to give to his countrymen—if this be the sum of a life of successful ambition and public honour—then, for myself, I should say, society is not likely to hold together long, for the people will not suffer mere selfishness in power, so soon as they know it to be hollow and weak." And he wanted to turn the conversation on the crisis in France.

"Nay! one moment, son of Danton by Charlotte Corday," we said, with a smile. "What, on earth, is the situation in France to us? We have no Empire here, and no revolutionists but you! But, as to _Lothair_, do you not see refinement in the life depicted? They are people of taste, there is plenty of wit, a turn for art; in a word, what is happily connoted by Culture!" We knew he would not like the word, but we wanted to "draw" him, as the young bloods do the President of the Board of Trade.

"Culture!" said our friend, quickly. "Not in any sense of the word that I know. It is true the external forms of life and the habits of the lounging class are not described with quite the vulgar ignor-

ance of fashionable novelists. There is certainly
much social grace, some cultivation of mind, and
plenty of wit in the society described. But so there
has been in almost every order on the eve of its
extinction. All the *belles marquises* and the fascinating *chevaliers* of *Œil-de-Bœuf* did not prevent
the Court of the Louis from being utterly rotten
and mean. And this is rotten and mean. Is the
mind in it cultivated to any intelligible end? Is
not the mere external parade of wealth dwelt on
till one nauseates? Does not the book reek with
the stifling fumes of gold, as when the idiot puts
rails of solid gold round the tomb which covers
his useless old bones? Is not the life vapid, aimless,
arrogant, as if the world and the human race
existed only to gratify its selfish whims? I do not
say that its whims are gross; but that they are
fatuously selfish."

"Come, come, good fellow, you are losing your
sense of a jest," said we. "Much radicalism doth
make thee dull. Why! do you suppose now that
Lothair is as serious and earnest as yourself? One
would fancy all radicals had a ballot-box in place
of a skull. Go, and have an operation (under
chloroform), and get the joke inserted into your
head! Have you never enjoyed a satire or a farce
at the play? Do you really think a man of genius,
who has fooled British society to the top of its
bent, is going down on his knees to his own puppet,
in his old age? Forbid it, human genius and successful ambition! Can you not see the exquisite fooling

of the characters in the comedy? Was ever such fatuous and yet genial self-importance as the Duke's—and from life they say—so racy when you know the facts! And did you miss that touch of the neighbouring gentry and yeomanry escorting the young goose home—goose, who is absolutely nothing but fabulously rich; so artfully prepared, you know, when you have been just shown the very inside of the amiable young jackanapes. Five hundred of the gentry on horseback, many of them 'gentlemen of high degree,' the county squirearchy! And all the high jinks of the county when the lad comes of age, as droll as the kowtowing to the emperor at Pekin. Is there a story about the Mikado of Japan as good as the games at Muriel? And the croquet match absorbing statesmen, and played exclusively by Dukes and Duchesses, with gold and ivory mallets! And the gold plate at Crecy House; and the reverences of the haughty Catholics to the Cardinal—Cardinal to the life, to the very fringe of his hat strings, a photograph, too absurd! and the pigeon which was proud of being shot by a Duke! and the lad who throws a sovereign to the cabman! and the marshalled retainers and obsequious lackeys moving ever noiselessly but actively in the background! O! friend of the people, or friend of man, if that was lost on you, we must be sorry for you. You are like a deaf man at the Opera. Why, it is like a scene in Japan! Turn it all into Japanese, say 'the Mikado' for 'Majestic Theme'; say 'Daimios' for dukes, put 'two-

sworded retainers' for footmen in plush, and lots
of male and female Japanese kissing the dust when
Satsuma rides forth, and, if you like, a *hari-kari*
instead of a London ball, and you have Lothair
in Japan, and British society, and its mighty aristocracy, and the whole brother-to-the-Sun-and-
Moon business under the grotesque etiquette of
those absurd Tartars. And do you not see how
artfully the fulsome and false style is contrived to
heighten the illusion of the whole preposterous
system? Why, there is nothing better in Voltaire
or Montesquieu. Do you take *Candide* and the
Lettres Persanes au pied de la lettre too, most
literal of mankind? What of Beaumarchais and
the immortal Barber? Do you suppose Figaro
does not see anything droll in the Count's *ménage*?
And when the Count asks him what he, the Count,
had done to merit all those felicities, and Figaro
says—*Monseigneur, vous vous êtes donné la peine
de naître*—do you think Figaro says that, like a
solemn fool, or like a man of wit, laughing in his
sleeve? What of Beaumarchais' comedies? Are
they not one long joke from beginning to end, and
a rare joke, too; ay, and one which made men
think, and bore fruit! Come and be a good, tame
Jacobin, and leave the League for to-night. Go
and see Mario and Gassier in *Il Barbiere*; read
Beaumarchais' play before dinner, and you will
then see the fun in *Lothair*!"

"Pish!" said our serious friend, who really
had an appointment at the League. "If it be all

a joke, that makes it worse. It is rather a prolonged
joke, if it be, and one which plain folk do not readily
see through. The world is ready to take all this
as a revelation in sober truth, from one who, by
his own account, has had special favour from what
you call the Majestic Theme. To pander to the
public taste is itself a vile thing, even though you
scorn them for swallowing your bait. To parade
(being a man in authority whom princes delight
to honour)—to parade a worthless type of life, with
a wink to the knowing that you are quite of their
mind, is not a great part. To worship a great State
with the knee and the lip, and sneer at it in your
heart, and sneer aloud, and sneering, pocket all its
good things, and grasp at its chief seats, is rather
worse, I take it, than stupidly to believe in it.
Figaro, no doubt, laughed at his patrons; but he
dearly loved their kitchen, and he pocketed their
ducats. And therefore he was a rogue, as well as a
slave. But I see no Figaro in the matter, and in
truth I have no time for talking now. I have an
appointment at a conference of reformers about
the land question—the land question in England,
not in Ireland. Perhaps, indeed, you are all right!
I know nothing of literature, and never read a
novel. Write a review in praise of *Lothair*, and
convert me!" and the stubborn reformer went off
to his meeting on the Land Question, and quite
forgot *Il Barbiere*, Beaumarchais, and *Lothair*.

"There was much truth, though, in his last
remark!" we said to ourselves, as he went off—

though it was impossible to avoid laughing at his serious air. But we took his advice about writing the Review, and we shall certainly send him a copy.

.　　.　　.　　.　　.

When our literal friend was gone off on his mission of pulling to pieces the majestic symmetry of our landed system, we fell into a reverie full of the witty Barber, and many a delightful reminiscence of M. Got at the Français, and Ronconi at the Opera. And then taking up *Lothair* to commence our review, we fell into a light sleep, and dreamt of the Barber!

O Figaro! O most audacious and deft of serving-men, what a wicked wit it is! What a society do you show us! What a sublime unconsciousness of its approaching end! How the young grandees of Spain work their own mad wills! What indescribable gambols of youth! What engaging liveliness of young blood! Any number of varlets to be had for a few ducats, and what droll puts the citizens seem in it all! A gallant lad gets into a scrape, which brings down Guard and Police! *Ecco! vien qui!* see the insignia of a Grandee! *Scusi Eccellenza:* I see! a thousand pardons! Off hats and up swords! *Le Roi s'amuse:*—make way there for his Grace! And all this our ingenious Beaumarchais had the happy idea of presenting to Paris in the last decade of the *ancien régime*. Bold playwright, have a care!

And the consummate impudence of our Figaro,

the exquisite liberties he takes with his great
friends! strutting behind their pompous footsteps,
mimicking their gait, and laughing back at the
audience. O mad wag, they will find thee out!
Why Bartolo's self, though thou art thrusting
thy lather into his rheumy old eyes, will see thou
art mocking! And as for Almaviva, he may be a
grandee of Spain, but he is a gentleman, Barber,
and may not relish thy menial pranks!

And what a rich and golden kind of life it is in
Almaviva's palaces, if you chance to live there;
how the power of wealth can create like a con-
juror's rod; what extravaganzas of caprice money
can produce!

> O che bel vivere,
> Che bel piacere,
> Per un Barbiere,
> Di qualitá—di qualitá!

All in good taste, too! from the best makers in
the *Puerta del Sol*—solid, real, representing so
much human labour, so many consumable things,
so much food, clothing, etc., as the dull dogs in
political economy make out; and the cream of
it is, that each production is more useless and
bizarre than the last. It is like an Arabian night
—Aladdin's lamp, Peribanou's fan. Ask for what
you like—there it is. Will his Lordship ride? See,
a troop of exquisite thoroughbred Barbs stand
pawing the turf, and champing their golden bits
whilst inimitable jockeys hold the stirrup! Would
his Grace care to sail? Haste! ten thousand

labourers, whilst thou art at luncheon, all carefully kept out of sight, shall make thee a spacious lake of artificial water: a gondola of wrought pearl floats on its perfumed breast—its sails are of amber satin. Will your Grace deign to take the trouble to sink into this velvet couch? Does his Highness like this prospect? Presto! a majestic palace rises with its stately saloons from out its statued terraces. His Grace's retainers throng its porches in obsequious crowds, and with the plumage of a cockatoo! Will his Lordship enter and deign to pass a day beneath the chaste magnificence of his new home? or will his Excellency condescend to indicate in which of his princely castles he will be served?

And the beauty of it is, that it is all real. It is fact. No Aladdin's palaces vanishing with the dream. But there they stand, built by actual human hands, and fitted up, as we say, by the best purveyors in Madrid. It is a little prosaic—it wants the romance of Aladdin; but it gains tenfold in being real. One of those economic bores would calculate out for you how much sweat of man went to the making of it all; how many millions of men and women it would support if it were all turned into food; how many lives have been worn out in attaining this stupendous result. And, after all, if your whim so be, you won't let the poor wretches even see you; but will go and hire lodgings in the Champs Elysées, or perhaps, after all, live in a tent on the top of Caucasus. O it beats Crassus and Lucullus, and dims Versailles and Monseigneurs!

And the best of it is, that it is all right and good
It is necessary to give a high tone to life. Authors,
statesmen, bishops even can prove it. Crassus was
a brute, Versailles was a blunder; but this—this
is the cultured magnificence of their stately lives.

What a dream we had! We seemed to see a
Magnifico—was it Figaro, Aladdin, Rouge Sang-
lier, or some Grand Vizier of all the cultured
magnificence of these stately lives?—(by special
behest of the Majestic Theme) enter into the
Paradise prepared for him of old. We beheld him
in a vision, bepalaced for evermore in choice saloons
resplendent with ormolu and scagliola! There, as
he reclined on couches of amber-satin, dazzling
duchesses and paladins of high degree fed him with
hatchis, as seraphic as his fancies; and served him
from salvers of sapphire, expressly manufactured
by Ruby of Bond Street. Farewell! Barber-Grand-
Vizier! in thy day thou hast amused many, apparently thyself also; why shouldest thou not
amuse us?

Moral! Retrorsum Tonsor! satis lusisti! Get
thee behind the scenes, Barber, and let another
speak the epilogue. The historian saith: " Small
substance in that Figaro: thin wire-drawn intrigues,
thin wire-drawn sentiments and sarcasms; a thing
lean, barren; yet which winds and whisks itself
as through a wholly mad universe, adroitly, with a
high-sniffing air; wherein each, which is the grand
secret, may see some image of himself and of his
own state and ways. So it runs its hundred nights,

and all France runs with it; laughing applause—
all men must laugh, and a horse-racing Anglo-
maniac noblesse loudest of all. . . . Beaumarchais
has now culminated, and unites the attributes of
several demigods." (Carlyle, *French Revolution*;
sub ann. 1784.)

CHRISTOPHER MARLOWE

By Edward Dowden

THE study of Shakespeare and his contemporaries is the study of one family consisting of many members, all of whom have the same life-blood in their veins, all of whom are recognisable by accent and bearing, and acquired habits, and various unconscious self-revealments as kinsmen, while each possesses a character of his own, and traits of mind and manners and expression which distinguish him from the rest. The interest of the study is chiefly in the gradual apprehension, now on this side, now on that, of the common nature of this great family of writers, until we are in complete intellectual possession of it, and in tracing out the characteristics peculiar to each of its individuals. There is, perhaps, no other body of literature towards which we are attracted by so much of unity, and at the same time by so much of variety. If the school of Rubens had been composed of greater men than it was, we should have had an illustrious parallel in the history of painting to the group of Shakespeare and his contemporaries in the history of poetry.

The "school of Rubens" we say; we could

hardly speak with accuracy of the "school of Shakespeare." Yet there can be little doubt that he was in a considerable degree the master of the inferior and younger artists who surrounded him. It is the independence of Ben Jonson's work and its thorough individuality, rather than comparative greatness or beauty of poetical achievement, which has given him a kind of acknowledged right to the second place amongst the Elizabethan dramatists, a title to vice-president's chair in the session of the poets. His aims were different from those of the others, and at a time when plays and playwrights were little esteemed, he had almost a nineteenth-century sense of the dignity of art, and of his own art in particular:

And he told them plainly he deserved the bays,
For his were called Works, where others were but Plays.

But Ford, and Webster, and Massinger, and Beaumont and Fletcher, and the rest (who were content, like Shakespeare, to write "plays," and did not aspire to "works") are really followers of the greatest of all dramatic writers, and very different handiwork they would probably have turned out had they wrought in their craft without the teaching of his practice and example. Shakespeare's immediate predecessors were men of no mean powers; but they are separated by a great gulf from his contemporaries and immediate successors. That tragedy is proportioned to something else than the number of slaughtered bodies

piled upon the stage at the end of Act Five, that
comedy has store of mirth more vital, deeper,
happier, more human than springs from

> Jigging veins of rhyming mother wits,
> And such conceits as clownage keeps in pay—

these were discoveries in art made by Shakespeare;
and is it too much to suppose that but for him these
discoveries might have come later by a dozen years
or thereabouts? The works of the pre-Shakespeareans are of small interest for the most part,
except as illustrating a necessary stage of growth
in the history of the drama. They do not win
upon us with the charm, the singleness of aim, the
divine innocency, the sacred inexperience, the unc-
tion of art, which we are sensible of in the works
of Raphael's predecessors. Italian painting may be
personified under the figure of a royal maiden who,
after a period of chaste seclusion and tender vir-
ginity, came forth into the world, and was a queen
and mother of men. The English drama was,
first, a schoolboy, taught rude piety by the priests,
and rude jokes by his fellows; then a young man,
lusty, passionate, mettlesome, riotous, aspiring,
friendly, full of extravagant notions and huffing
words, given to irregular ways and disastrous
chances and desperate recoveries, but, like Shakespeare's wild prince, containing the promise of that
grave, deep-thoughted, and magnificent manhood
which was afterwards realised.

It is, however, amongst the pre-Shakespeareans

that we find the man who, of all the Elizabethan dramatists, stands next to Shakespeare in poetical stature, the one man who, if he had lived longer and accomplished the work which lay clear before him, might have stood even *beside* Shakespeare, as supreme in a different province of dramatic art. Shakespeare would have been master of the realists or naturalists; Marlowe, master of the idealists. The starting-point of Shakespeare, and of those who resemble him, is always something concrete, something real in the moral world—a human character; to no more elementary components than human characters can the products of their art be reduced in the alembic of critical analysis; further than these they are irreducible. The starting-point of Marlowe, and of those who resemble Marlowe, is something abstract—a passion or an idea; to a passion or an idea each work of theirs can be brought back. Revenge is not the subject of the *Merchant of Venice*; Antonio and Shylock, Portia and Nerissa, Lorenzo and Jessica, Bassanio and Gratiano—these are the true subjects. Even of *Romeo and Juliet* the subject is not love, but two young and loving hearts surrounded by a group of most living figures, and over-shadowed by a tyrannous fate. Those critics, and they are unfortunately the most numerous since German criticism became a power in this country, who attempt to discover an intention, idea, or, as they say, *motiv* presiding throughout each of Shakespeare's plays, have got upon an entirely mistaken

track, and they inevitably come out after laby-
rinthine wanderings at the other end of nowhere.
Shakespeare's trade was not that of preparing nuts
with concealed mottoes and sentiments in them for
German commentators to crack. Goethe, who
wrought in Shakespeare's manner (though sometimes with a self-consciousness which went hanker-
ing after ideas and intentions), Goethe saw clearly
the futility of all attempts to release from their
obscurity the secrets of his own works, as if the
mystery of what he had created were other than
the mystery of life. The children of his imagination
were bone of his bone, and flesh of his flesh, not
constructions of his intellect nor embodied types
of the passions. "*Wilhelm Meister* is one of the
most incalculable productions"—it is Goethe
himself who is speaking—" I myself can scarcely
be said to have the key to it. People seek a central
point, and that is hard and not even right. I should
think a rich manifold life brought close to our eyes
would be enough in itself without any express
tendency, which, after all, is only for the intellect."
A rich manifold life brought close to our eyes—that
is the simplest and truest account possible of any
or all of Shakespeare's dramas. But Marlowe
worked, as Milton also worked, from the starting-
point of an idea or passion, and the critic who might
dissect all the creatures of Shakespeare's art without
ever having the honour to discover a soul, may
really, by dexterous anatomy, come upon the souls
of Marlowe's or of Milton's creatures—intelligent

monads somewhere seated observant in the pineal gland.

Shakespeare and Marlowe, the two foremost men of the Elizabethan artistic movement, remind us in not a few particulars of the two foremost men of the artistic movement in Germany seventy or eighty years ago, Goethe and Schiller. Shakespeare and Goethe are incomparably the larger and richer natures, their art is incomparably the greater and more fruitful; yet they were themselves much greater than their art. Shakespeare rendered more by a measureless sum of a man's whole nature into poetry than Marlowe did; yet his own life ran on below the rendering of it into poetry, and was never wholly absorbed and lost therein. We can believe that under different circumstances Shakespeare might never have written a line, might have carried all that lay within him unuttered to his grave. When quite a young man, and winning great rewards of fame, he could lay aside his pen entirely for a time, as when Spenser lamented:

Our pleasant Willy, ah! is dead of late,

and, while still in the full manhood of his powers, he chose to put off his garments of enchantment, break his magic staff, and dismiss his airy spirits; or, in plain words, bring to a close his career as poet, and live out the rest of his life as country gentleman in his native town. It is a suggestive fact, too, that the scattered references to Shakespeare which we find in the writings of his contemporaries, show us the poet concealed and almost forgotten in the man, and make it clear that he moved among his fellows with no assuming of the bard or prophet, no aspect as of one inspired, no air of authority as of one divinely commissioned; that, on the contrary, he appeared as a pleasant comrade, genial, gentle, full of civility in the large meaning of that word, upright in dealing, ready and bright in wit, quick and sportive in conversation. Goethe, also, though he valued his own works highly, valued them from a superior position as one above them, and independent of them. But Marlowe, like Schiller, seems to have lived in and for his art. His poetry was no episode in his life, but his very life itself. With an university education, and a prospect, which for a man of his powers can hardly have been an unpromising one, of success in one of the learned professions (not necessarily the Church), he must abandon his hardly-earned advantages, return to the poverty from which he had sprung, and add to poverty the disgrace of an actor's and playwright's life. His contemporaries usually speak of him as a man would be spoken of who was possessed by his art, rather than as one who, like Shakespeare, held it in possession.

> That fine madness still he did retain,
> Which rightly should possess a poet's brain.

So wrote Drayton; and according to Chapman's fine hyperbole he

> Stood
> Up to the chin in the Pierian flood.

This is not the way in which Shakespeare is spoken of. Nor is it an uncharacteristic circumstance that probably while he lay for a short time tortured with the wound of his own dagger, and death was hastening, one of Marlowe's chief anxieties was about the fate of his *Hero and Leander,* and that he commended it for completion to the man of all others best fitted for the task—the great translator of Homer, whose words have just been quoted.

But if Marlowe is the Schiller—the subjective poet, the idealist, as Shakespeare is the Goethe, objective and naturalistic, of Elizabethan art—he is a Schiller of a decidedly Satanic school. With an important critical movement behind him, around him a regulated state of society, and many influences calling into activity the better part of his nature, the true Schiller's head and heart and sensibilities as an artist passed through their "Sturm und Drang" fever, and came forth illuminated, purified, and elevated. On the other hand, the world amidst which he moved was too much one of merely cultured refinement; no rude but large and ardent popular heart beat in his hearing; rather, in the court and *salons* and theatre of Weimar, official waistcoats rose and fell with admirable but not very inspiring regularity over self-possessed and irreproachable bosoms. The talk was of poems, pictures, busts, medals, and the last little new law of the Duke. It is not surprising that Schiller's art should have a touch of coldness in it. Marlowe had behind him, not a critical movement like the German, but the glare of Smithfield fires and the ghostly procession of noble figures dealt with by the headsman on Tower Hill, terrible religious and political battles, and the downfall of a faith. For his own part, taking art as the object of his devotion, he thrust all religions somewhat fiercely aside, and professed an angry Atheism. The Catholic hierarchy and creed he seems to have hated with an energy profoundly different from the feeling of Shakespeare, distinguished as that was by a discriminating justice. The reckless Bohemian London life which Marlowe shared with his companions, Greene, Lodge, Nash, and other wild livers, had nothing in it to sober his judgment, to chasten and purify his imagination and taste, nothing or very little to elevate his feelings, But it was quick and passionate. The "Sturm und Drang" through which our English dramatists passed was of far sterner stress than that of Germany. But Marlowe did pass through it. He perished unhappily before he had acquired mastery in his second style. He lived long enough to escape from the period, so to speak, of his *Robbers*, not long enough to attain to the serene ideality of a *Wilhelm Tell*. But Marlowe possessed one immense advantage over Schiller—he stood not in the midst of a petty ducal court, but in the centre of a great nation, and at a time when that nation was all air and fire, its baser elements disappearing in the consciousness of new-found power, a time when the nation was no aggregation of atoms cohering by accident, and each clamorous for its own particular rights, but a living body, with something like a unity of ideas, and with feelings self-organised around splendid objects of common interest, pride, and admiration. The strength and weakness of what Marlowe accomplished in literature correspond with the influences from the real world to which he was subject. He is great, ardent, aspiring; but he is also without balance, immoderate, unequal, extravagant. There is an artistic grace which is the counterpart of the theological grace of charity. It pervades everything that Shakespeare has written; there is little of it in Marlowe's writings. There is in them " a hunger and thirst after unrighteousness, a glow of the imagination unhallowed by anything but its own energies. His thoughts burn within him like a furnace with bickering flames, or throwing out black smoke and mists that hide the dawn of genius, or like a poisonous mineral corrode the heart." [1] If a Schiller, then, surely a Schiller of a Satanic school.

Marlowe's works consist of six or seven plays and some translations, one of which—a paraphrase of the *Hero and Leander* of the pseudo-Musæus —is remarkable as evidencing, more than any other of his writings, the thoroughly Renaissance feeling for sensuous beauty which Marlowe possessed in a degree hardly less than that displayed by Shakespeare in his youthful *Venus and Adonis*. Of the

[1] Hazlitt.

dramas, one was produced in conjunction with
Nash, and we cannot safely assign to its authors
their respective shares in the work. One—*The
Massacre at Paris*—seems to have been thrown
off to meet some temporary occasion; and certainly,
however this may have been, it may without re-
morse be set down as worthless. A third was written,
we can hardly doubt, when the poet was in the
transition period from his early to what would have
been, if he had lived, his mature style. It is in
truth the least characteristic of all his more important writings. There are critics who can more
readily forgive any literary deficiencies or incapa-
cities than sins of actual commission, who can bear
with every evidence of dulness of poetical vision,
languor of the thinking power, uncertainty of the
shaping hands, and constitutional asthenia, but
who have no toleration for splendid crimes, broad-
blown sins of the sanguine temperament, extravagant
fancies, thoughts that climb too high, turbulency
of manner, and great swelling words of vanity.
These have pronounced *Edward the Second* Marlowe's best play. And it is, doubtless, free from the
violence and extravagance of the dramas that
preceded it, from the vaulting ambition of poetical
style, which " o'erleaps itself, and falls o' the
other "; but, except in a few scenes, and notably
the closing ones, it wants also the clear raptures,
the high reaches of wit, the " brave translunary
things," the single lines—each one enough to
ransom a poet from captivity—which especially

characterise Marlowe. The historical matter he is unable to handle as successfully as a subject of an imaginative or partly mythical kind; it does not yield and take shape in his hands as readily, and accordingly *Edward the Second,* though containing a few splendid passages, is rather a series of scenes from the chronicles of England than a drama.

Three plays remain,[1] and on these the fame of Marlowe must rest—*Tamburlaine the Great, The Tragical History of Dr. Faustus,* and *The Jew of Malta.* Each of these is admirably characteristic, and could have proceeded from no other brain than that of its creator. The three together form a great achievement in literature for a man probably not more than twenty-seven years of age when the latest was written; and they still stand apart from the neighbouring crowd of dramatic compositions, and close to one another—a little group distinguished by peculiar marks of closest kinship, a physiognomy, and complexion, and demeanour, and accent of their own. Each of the three is the rendering into artistic form of the workings of a single passion, while at the same time each of these several passions is only a different form of life assumed by one supreme passion, central in all the great characters of Marlowe, magisterial, claiming the whole man, and in its operation fatal.

The subject of *Tamburlaine*—probably Mar-

---

[1] Four, if we count separately the two parts of *Tamburlaine.*

lowe's earliest work, certainly the first which made
an impression on the public—if we would express
it in the simplest way, is the mere lust of dominion,
the passion of "a mighty hunter before the Lord"
for sovereign sway, the love of power in its crudest
shape. This, and this alone, living and acting in
the person of the Scythian shepherd, gives unity
to the multitude of scenes which grow up before
us and fall away, like the fiery-hearted blossoms
of some inexhaustible tropical plant, blown with
sudden and strong desire, fading and dropping away
at night, and replaced next morning by others as
sanguine and heavy with perfume. There is no
construction in *Tamburlaine*. Instead of two plays
there might as well have been twenty, if Marlowe
could have found it in his heart to husband his
large supply of kings, emperors, soldans, pashas,
governors, and viceroys who perish before the
Scourge of God, or had he been able to discover
empires, provinces, and principalities with which
to endow a new race of rulers. The play ends from
sheer exhaustion of resources. As Alexander was
reduced to weep for another world to conquer,
so Tamburlaine might have wept because there
were no more emperors to fill his cages, no more
monarchs to increase his royal stud. He does not
weep, but what is much better, dies. The play
resembles in its movement no other so much as
the *Sultan Amurath* of De Quincey's elder brother.
"What by the bowstring, and what by the scimitar,
the sultan had so thinned the population with

which he commenced business that scarcely any of the characters remained alive at the end of Act the first." Five crops had to be taken off the ground in the tragedy, amounting, in short, to five tragedies involved in one. The difference is, that Marlowe could not be satisfied with less than ten crops and a corresponding number of tragedies.

Yet *Tamburlaine* is the work of a master-hand, untrained. If from some painting ill-composed, full of crude and violent colour, containing abundant proofs of weakness and inexperience, and having half its canvas crowded with extravagant grotesques which the artist took for sublime—if from such a painting one wonderful face looked out at us, the soul in its eyes and on its lips, a single desire possessing it, eager and simple as a flame, should we question the genius of the painter? And somewhat in this manner the single passion which has the hero of the piece for its temporary body and instrument looks out at us from the play of *Tamburlaine*. The lust and the pride of conquest, the ambition to be a god upon earth, the confident sense that in one's own will resides the prime force of nature, disdain of each single thing, how splendid soever, which the world can offer by way of gift or bribe, because less than the possession of all seems worthless—these are feelings which, though evidence from history that they are real is not wanting, are yet even imagined in a vivid way by very few persons. The demands which most of us make on life are moderate; our little lives run on with few great ambitions, and this gross kind of ambition is peculiarly out of relation to our habits of desire. But Marlowe, the son of the Canterbury shoemaker, realised in imagination this ambition as if it were his very own, and gave it most living expression; most sincere and natural expression also. The author of *Faustus* and *The Jew of Malta* is wholly in such lines as these of Tamburlaine, spoken while he was yet a mere fortunate adventurer:

> But, since they measure our deserts so mean,
> That in conceit bear empires on our spears,
> Affecting thoughts coequal with the clouds,
> They shall be kept our forced followers
> Till with their eyes they view us Emperors.

And these:

> Forsake thy king, and do but join with me,
> And we will triumph over all the world;
> I hold the Fates fast bound in iron chains,
> And with my hand turn Fortune's wheel about.

And these spoken of Tamburlaine by Meander:

> Some powers divine, or else infernal, mix'd
> Their angry seeds at his conception;
> For he was never sprung of human race,
> Since with the spirit of his fearful pride
> He dares so doubtlessly resolve of rule,
> And by profession be ambitious.

And lastly these, Tamburlaine speaking:

> Nature that fram'd us of four elements
> Warring within our breasts for regiment,
> Doth teach us all to have aspiring minds:
> Our souls, whose faculties can comprehend
> The wondrous architecture of the world,
> And measure every wandering planet's course,
> Still climbing after knowledge infinite,

And always moving as the restless spheres
Will us to wear ourselves, and never rest
Until we reach the ripest fruit of all,
That perfect bliss and sole felicity,
The sweet fruition of an earthly crown.

There is something gross in this ambition, this thirst for reign, this gloating over " the sweetness of a crown," but the very excess or transcendency of the passion saves it from vulgarity. The love of pomp is not the mean love of pomp, but the imperial, combined with the self-surrender of the Renaissance poet to the lust of the eye and the pride of life. Command over material display and pageantry, from the " copper-laced coat and crimson velvet breeches " of the Conqueror up to the " pampered jades of Asia," is valued chiefly as an emblem of triumph and of power, or rather as a fragment of that universal power which sways all things to its will, and suggestive of it. It is a fine piece of consistency preserved in resistance to the temptation of stage moralising, that when Tamburlaine's great career draws towards its close, and he sees the world passing away from his grasp, he does not lose faith in the kingdoms of the world and their glory. He knows that he must submit to the tyranny of Death; he exhorts his sons to the acquiring of

that magnanimity
That nobly must admit necessity;

life, he sees, is transitory, but he does not despise it for its transitoriness; sovereignty must be resigned, but still he is proud that he was Tamburlaine and a king; and he delivers over the possession of his empire to his children, lamenting only that their "sweet desires," and those of his friends, must henceforth be deprived of his company. There is a severity of conception in this scene of Tamburlaine's death, which was attained through the projection into his art of Marlowe's own exceeding pride of will.

In one of the passages quoted above the reader may have been struck by the fine line in which our souls are spoken of as "still climbing after knowledge infinite." That aspiring, insatiate, and insatiable curiosity, which for our generation Mr. Browning has endeavoured to represent in the person of Paracelsus, Marlowe also conceived in his own way, and with characteristic energy. Faustus is the Paracelsus of Marlowe. Over the soul of the Würtemberg doctor the passion for knowledge dominates, and all influences of good and evil, the voices of damned and of blessed angels reach him faint and ineffectual as dreams, or distant music, or the suggestions of long-forgotten odours, save as they promise something to glut the fierce hunger and thirst of his intellect. All subjects, however, in the stream of Marlowe's genius are hurried in a single direction. Pride of will drew to itself all other forces of his nature, and made them secondary and subordinate; and accordingly we are not surprised when we find that, in Marlowe's hands, the passion for knowledge which possesses Faustus becomes little more than a body, as it were,

giving a special form of life to the same consuming
lust of power which he had treated in the earlier
drama of *Tamburlaine*. To Faustus, in the suggestion of the Tempter, the words "knowing
good and evil" grow dim in the unhallowed
splendour of the promise "Ye shall be as gods."
All secrets of Nature and of Fate he desires to
penetrate, but not in order that he may contem-
plate their mysteries in philosophic calmness, not
that he may possess his soul in the serene light of
ascertained primal truths; rather it is for the lordship over men and things which knowledge places
in his hands that he chiefly desires it. Logic, law,
physic, divinity, have yielded their whole stores
into his keeping, but they have left his intellect
unsatisfied, craving for acquisitions of a less formal,
a more natural and living kind, and they have
afforded him no adequate field, and feeble instruments for the display of the forces of his will. It
is magic which with every discovery to the intellect
unites a corresponding gift of power:

> 'Tis magic, magic that hath ravished me.

What is knowledge worth if it does not enable him
to obtain mastery over gross matter, over the lives
and fortunes of men, over the elements of air and
earth, of fire and water, and over the strong ele-
mental spirits? To be surrounded with proofs
and witnesses of the transcendent might of his own
will,—this is the ultimate desire of Faustus, as in
other circumstances and seeking other manifestations,

it was of Tamburlaine. But the scholar does not ever disappear in the magician. In the first heated vision of the various objects towards which the new agency at his command might be turned, projects rise before him of circling Germany with brass, of driving the Prince of Parma from the land, and reigning "sole king of all the provinces"; yet even in that hour there mingle with more vulgar ambitions the ambitions of the thinker and the student; he would have his subject spirits resolve him of all ambiguities, and read to him strange philosophies. The pleasure, which afterwards he seeks, less for its own sake than to banish the hated thought of the approaching future, is the quintessence of pleasure. He is not made for coarse delights. He desires no beauty but that of "the fairest maid in Germany," or the beauty of Helen of Troy:

> Was this the face that launch'd a thousand ships,
> And burnt the topless towers of Ilium?
> Sweet Helen, make me immortal with a kiss.

He chooses no song but Homer's song, no music but that of Amphion's harp:

> Long ere this I should have slain myself
> Had not sweet pleasure conquer'd deep despair.
> Have not I made blind Homer sing to me
> Of Alexander's love and Œnon's death?
> And hath not he that built the walls of Thebes,
> With ravishing sound of his melodious harp,
> Made music with my Mephistophilis?

And in the scene of parting with the two scholars, immediately preceding the uncompanioned agony of the doomed man's latest hour—a scene distinguished by a lofty pathos which we find nowhere else in Marlowe—there is throughout an atmosphere of learning, of refinement, of scholarly urbanity, which makes us feel how thoroughly Marlowe had preserved his original conception of the character of Faustus, even while he degraded him to the low conjurer of certain passages, introduced by a writer singularly devoid of humour, to make sport for the groundlings of the theatre.

A grosser air is breathed throughout *The Jew of Malta*. The whole play is murky with smoke of the pit. Evil desires, evil thoughts, evil living, fill its five acts to the full. Nine-tenths of the picture are as darkly shadowed as some shadowy painting of Rembrandt; but, as might also be in one of Rembrandt's paintings, in the centre there is a head relieved against the gloom, lit by what strange light we do not know, unless it be the reflection from piles of gold and gems—a head fascinating and detestable, of majestic proportions, full of intellect, full of malice and deceit, with wrinkled brow, beak-like nose, cruel lips, and eyes that, though half-hooded by leathery lids, triumph visibly in the success of something devilish. Barabas is the dedicated child of sin from his mother's womb. As he grew in stature he must have grown in crooked wisdom and in wickedness. His heart is a nest where there is room for the patrons of the seven deadly sins to lodge, but one chief devil is its permanent occupier—Mammon. The lust of money is the passion of the Jew, which is constantly awake and active. His bags are the children of his bowels, more loved than his Abigail, and the dearer because they were begotten through deceit or by violence. Yet Barabas is a superb figure. His energy of will is so great; his resources and inventions are so inexhaustible; he is so illustrious a representative of material power and of intellectual. Even his love of money has something in it of sublime, it is so huge a desire. He is no miser treasuring each contemptible coin. Precisely as Tamburlaine looked down with scorn at all ordinary kingships and lordships of the earth, as Faustus held for worthless the whole sum of stored-up human learning in comparison with the infinite knowledge to which he aspired, so Barabas treats with genuine disdain the opulence of common men. The play opens, as *Faustus* does, in an impressive way, discovering the merchant alone in his counting-house, flattering his own sense of power with the sight of his possessions. He sits in the centre of a vast web of commercial enterprises, controlling and directing them all. Spain, Persia, Araby, Egypt, India, are tributary to the Jew. He holds hands with the Christian governor of the island. By money he has become a lord of men, as Tamburlaine did by force, and Faustus by knowledge, and the winds and the seas that bear his argosies about are his ministers.

It is obvious that the lust of money, and the power that comes by money, form the subject of

The Jew of Malta. We should indeed be straining matters, accommodating them to gain for our exposition an artistic completeness, if we were to say that Barabas desires money only for the power which its possession confers. This, in his worship of gold, is certainly a chief element, but he loves it also for its own sake with a fond extravagance. In the dawn after that night when Abigail rescued his treasures from their hiding-place in his former dwelling, now converted into a Christian nunnery, the old raven hovers amorously over his recovered bags, and sings above them as a lark does above her young. Yet still it is the sense of power regained which puts the sweetest drop into his cup of bliss:

> O my girl,
> My gold, my fortune, my felicity,
> Strength to my soul, death to mine enemy!
> Welcome the first beginner of my bliss.

But Marlowe found means in another way to gratify in this play his own passion for power, his pride in the display of the puissance of human will. The opening scene, in which the Jew appears as a great master in the art of money-getting, and surrounded by the works of his hands, in which he is proud, secure, and happy, is quickly succeeded by others in which he is seen stripped of his wealth, turned out of doors by Christian tyranny, and exposed to common ignominy and insult. The rest of the drama is occupied with the great game which Barabas plays, first against his Christian persecutors, afterwards against his own daughter allied with them, and his dangerous tool Ithamore, the cut-throat slave whom he has bought. His hand is henceforth against every man, and every man's hand against him. When he is hunted he doubles on his pursuers, and for a while escapes; any swine-eating dog that comes too close gets a shrewd bite which stops his cry, and at last, when brought to bay, and when his supreme design has failed by counter-treachery, when fairly hunted down, he turns fiercely on his opponents, is still master of himself and of the situation, and rises above those who watch his death by the grandeur of his resolution.

It has not seemed necessary here to dwell upon all that is worthless, and worse than worthless, in Marlowe's plays—on the " midsummer madness " of *Tamburlaine*, the contemptible buffoonery of *Dr. Faustus*, and the overloaded sensational atrocities of *The Jew of Malta*. Such criticism everyone but an Ancient Pistol does for himself. We all recognise the fustian of Marlowe's style, and the ill effects of the demands made upon him by sixteenth-century playgoers for such harlequinade as they could appreciate. A more important thing to recognise is that up to the last Marlowe's great powers were ripening, while his judgment was becoming sane, and his taste purer. He was escaping, as has been already said, from his " Sturm und Drang " when he was lost to the world. *Tamburlaine* was written at the age of twenty-two, *Faustus* two or three years later. At such an age accomplishment is rare; we usually look for no more than promise. If Shakespeare had died at the age when Marlowe died we should have known little of the capacity which lay within him of creating a Macbeth, a Lear, an Othello, a Cleopatra. Marlowe has left us three great ideal figures of Titanic strength and size. That we should say is much. In one particular a most important advance from *Tamburlaine* to *Dr. Faustus* and the later plays is discernible—in versification. His contemporaries appear to have been much impressed by the greatness of his verse—Marlowe's "mighty line"; and it was in the tirades of *Tamburlaine* that blank verse was first heard upon a public stage in England. But in this play the blank verse is like a gorgeous robe of brocade, stiff with golden embroidery; afterwards in his hands it becomes pliable, and falls around the thought or feeling which it covers in nobly significant lines.

Had Marlowe lived longer we may surmise, with some degree of assurance, one, at least, of the subjects which would have engaged his attention —the lust of beauty and the power of beauty. There is very little of amatory writing in any of his plays except that written in conjunction with Nash. Tender love-making of the idyllic or romantic kind Marlowe was little fitted to represent. But we have the clearest evidence from scattered passages that Marlowe had conceived the tyrannous power of beauty in that transcendent way in which he conceived other forms of power   It is sufficient

EDWARD DOWDEN

to remind the reader of the scene in which Helena
rises before Faustus. And there is one passage in
Tamburlaine which in itself is quite enough to
show us that the passionate desire of beauty in its
most ideal form was not inexperienced by the poet:

> What is beauty, saith my sufferings, then?
> If all the pens that ever poets held
> Had fed the feeling of their masters' thoughts,
> And every sweetness that inspired their hearts,
> Their minds, and muses on admirèd themes;
> If all the heavenly quintessence they still
> From their immortal flowers of poesy,
> Wherein, as in a mirror, we perceive
> The highest reaches of a human wit;
> If these had made one poem's period,
> And all combin'd in beauty's worthiness,
> Yet should there hover in their restless heads,
> One thought, one grace, one wonder, at the least,
> Which into words no virtue can digest.

If another passage in *Tamburlaine*:

> Still climbing after knowledge infinite,

announced the poet's Paracelsus, does not this
more distinctly announce his never-created Aprile?

PRINTED BY
THE TEMPLE PRESS AT LETCHWORTH IN GREAT BRITAIN